Jeff,

it's an honor to share these stories of life,

Warmly,
Rita
xox

STORIES

FROM A
TEACHER'S HEART

MEMORIES
OF LOVE,
LIFE,
AND FAMILY

RITA M. WIRTZ, MA

LifeRich Publishing is a registered trademark of The Reader's Digest Association, Inc.

LifeRich Publishing books may be ordered through booksellers or by contacting:

LifeRich Publishing
1663 Liberty Drive
Bloomington, IN 47403
www.liferichpublishing.com
1 (888) 238-8637

Because of the dynamic nature of the Internet, any web addresses or links contained in this book may have changed since publication and may no longer be valid. The views expressed in this work are solely those of the author and do not necessarily reflect the views of the publisher, and the publisher hereby disclaims any responsibility for them.

Any people depicted in stock imagery provided by Getty Images are models, and such images are being used for illustrative purposes only.
Certain stock imagery © Getty Images.

ISBN: 978-1-4897-2162-4 (sc)
ISBN: 978-1-4897-2163-1 (hc)
ISBN: 978-1-4897-2161-7 (e)

Library of Congress Control Number: 2019933935

Print information available on the last page.

LifeRich Publishing rev. date: 04/25/2019

DEDICATION

My stories are dedicated to my dearest friend, Estelle Werve, in loving memory.

And then she was gone. But not forgotten. 2018.

I met her in 1991, a long time ago.

As Keynoter and Seminar leader for California School Boards Association Boardsmanship Academy, I met a lot of really great community leaders. I recall looking out at the audience and seeing a lady about my age, a shrimp like me, with a dark, 'Miss Edna-like' short haircut, big eyes, and an infectious sense of humor about her.

Estelle was a pint-sized dynamo.

Yes, Estelle stood out in that large audience. I don't remember what activity I was doing, but I recall seeing Estelle, arms across her chest, laughing and smiling pretty much simultaneously. Then she asked a question, and I knew she really knew her stuff. She had a very cool voice.

By coincidence, leaving for home, we met at the airport and found out we were on the same plane back to Sacramento. And so it began. Estelle and I were solid friends, with her husband, Don, my dear friend added into the mix. Fortunately, my late husband William adored them both so it was easy to spend time together, first in Sacramento, later at our mountain cabin home.

Estelle was an extraordinary school board member for sixteen years, in one of the largest school districts in California. She was president of the board for four terms. I observed her visiting classrooms regularly at all district schools, routinely listening and advising everybody on campuses, including principals, staffs, parents, and kiddos. She treated everyone the same, with respect and dignity.

Speaking of kiddos, Estelle excelled hanging out and teaching in classrooms at all levels. Astonishing, she never said a negative word about anybody she came in contact with, whether adults or students, parents or administrators.

Never retiring, Estelle was a role model for us all. She continued to substitute-teach all over the place and excelled wherever she went, her 'Miss Edna' fan club sprouting all over like the famed bamboo plant.

Estelle and Don were married for an extraordinary number of years. Estelle was also a loving mother, aunt, grandma, and friend. Everybody felt her light. Everybody.

Student. Learner. Teacher. We are all teachers, really, motivating and inspiring one another, and Estelle was right in the middle of that loop of learning-love. Because of her action and passion, returning to school when others were long done, long gone from classrooms and kiddos, Estelle was just starting out. Estelle showed her tenacity, succeeding at whatever task she took on.

Continually modeling for everybody what love and equity could look like, one step at a time: that was Estelle's gift.

Estelle had a number of university degrees, beginning with a social studies degree from California State University, a bunch learned in the school of life, too. Always a lifelong learner, Estelle's burning desire and curiosity reached the master's degree level, in second language learning, multicultural education, curriculum, and instruction.

After I moved to Eugene, Estelle and I talked and corresponded. But at the very end, when I had no idea it was to be the end, and I was in the midst of just surviving, Estelle coached me on.

I'm here. She left. There is simply no way I can convey to you the depths of my angst and loss of Estelle. She was a rock and anchor, a joy to be around, for so many years.

The least I can do is dedicate this work of life and love to you, Estelle, and Don. I compiled my stories about education, equity and fairness, family and friends, schools, reading and literacy; all the things you cared about.

Because you stood up to be counted, to the last, even if you needed to stand on a chair, may your inspiration shine a glowing light to all who pick up this book and pass on whatever goodness, to countless others.

Love, Rita

Epigraph

Never doubt that a small group of thoughtful, committed citizens can change the world. Indeed, it's the only thing that ever has.

Margaret Mead (1901–1978)
Cultural anthropologist, researcher, and author

FOREWORD

Twenty-five years ago I was introduced to Rita by my late wife, Estelle, a recently-elected board member of a large local northern California unified school district. My wife attended the multifaceted Masters in Boardsmanship Academy offered by the California School Board Association to train new members in School Operations and Administration. Rita, the Keynote Speaker, was conducting one of the major seminars.

My wife thought I might help Rita structure a book she was preparing to supplement a seminar series, *Reading Champions*, for national presentation, as I was, and still am a professional writer, editor, and publisher. That turned out to be a six-month-long project, followed by three years of upper-division University study, and three more years of post-graduate work with Rita as my "coach," filling in the gaps left out of the "standard" curricula.

As I continued working with Rita, the immense expanse of her knowledge of teaching and structured education never ceased to amaze me. She was not only a teacher of children, she was, and is, a teacher of teachers—taking her in-depth knowledge of the science of teaching into way over five hundred classrooms across the country.

Our experience and methodology started to come together for the next-level book, *Reading Champs,* and covering the entire academic range from Preschool-through-High School and technical workplace, education. And I am living proof she has never stopped learning and teaching. But, then, Rita never stops growing. While most of us are retiring, planning on retiring, or wishing we could retire, Rita continues to roll along her road as an educational activist. Yet even there, she is active as a volunteer in preschool and elementary classrooms, constantly developing and producing new and better ways to reach children.

So now she has taken on the telling of stories of challenges and rewards encountered in her nearly half-a-century of building her extended family of students, whose lives she has influenced at the classroom level; teaching teachers, conducting numerous seminars, and tutoring 'hard to reach' students. In particular, these collected stories highlight Rita's recent achievements, life as a widow, mother, seeker, and learner.

Her secret in reaching the hard ones: "A child will usually blossom in an environment with a caring, loving, and patient teacher. Never forget that our environments are always going to be teaching us, for good or not so good, by example."

We need more involved people like Rita M. Wirtz—men and women, mothers and fathers, youth group leaders, who are willing to take on the challenge of preparing our children to become our nation's future leaders and teachers for at least the next fifty years. There is not, nor can there be, any more important call to action!

This is a book about seemingly small problems, and seemingly easy solutions, to potholes in our educational highways. Like Rita, you are the readers who can make all the difference in a child's and adult's life.

Get comfy, sit back, and select a story or two, then another, and another. This book is sure to warm your heart, make you think, and inspire you.

Donald E. Werve, Jr., M.Ed.

PREFACE

I never planned to be a widow.

I never wanted to join that club. Yet here I am, seven years of being alone, finding myself, as the saying goes. I am certainly not done yet, but this book provided a lot of growth. Continually in transitions, most unexpected, most unwelcome at first, then later, a different story.

That's what this book is all about: essays, brief staccato-like stories of my life as teacher, mother, family member, and educational activist of sorts. Yes, cancer survivor and widow. But there's more, of course.

I never thought of myself as an educational activist until recently when I read that about me. Yes, it does make sense now. But I never intended it to be so.

That being said, allow me to give you the backstory how this book came to be.

For a number of years after my husband William retired, we lived in a historic cabin home in the foothill mountains enroute Lake Tahoe. I was Keynoting, making special appearances, teaching credential reading courses, and working on my last book, *Reading Champs; Teaching Reading Made Easy*.

Homeschooling was very big in that community. One of my former Chapman University Credential students, Pam Laird, was in charge of the program. As a favor, I prepared several workshops for parents. I learned so much and had a wonderful time.

Of course, I met a number of children who needed reading help, so before I knew it, there I was, teaching and tutoring about thirty kids, homeschoolers, native American Miwok children, school kids in the bottom percentiles, acting-out kids, etc. It was a truly inspiring experience.

Then my husband became ill, and for the next six years I cared for him, with difficulty, living so far out. I managed to teach university courses and kids for a couple more years, but left my *Reading Champs* drafts sit on the shelf.

After I lost Bill, my friend Don Werve suggested I pick up the book again and we managed to finish it together. I finally decided to leave my mountain paradise to move to Eugene, Oregon. I have a large extended family and love all my kids, but Eugene became home. Bill had attended the University of Oregon in Eugene, as did my niece, Beth. My daughter, Rebecca, son-in law, TJ, and granddaughter, Morgan, were living in Eugene, so that was that.

I moved three times in four years—and may be moving again. I am a 'nester' so this has been a most challenging life transition: coming to Eugene, deciding where and how to live the rest of my life. Big stuff.

When I finally finished a polished edition of *Reading Champs*, I marketed it for a little while, and then left it sitting on a shelf again—this time, up on Amazon. I was more interested in getting back into the classroom one last time, and learning social media to leave my mark and legacy without traveling around the country anymore, lugging a big training trunk filled with goodies for teachers and classrooms. How did I ever do that?

I volunteered at the same preschool my granddaughter attended, an extraordinary setting for precious young learners. Through a literacy grant, a position opened up, I applied, and for a couple years—until illness struck—I savored learning how to teach the tiniest young learners and pre-readers from my new mentors.

I've been in Eugene over four years now. It seems like I moved here yesterday. Currently, I am living in a townhouse right on the Willamette River, quite enchanting. This transition gave me a chance to heal from the scourge of cancer and develop a notion that the blogs I had been writing might have greater meaning than I thought at the time I wrote each.

I happened to have a publicist for *Reading Champs* who encouraged me to respond with a 'yes' to Rae Pica, cofounder of BAM Radio Network. Way back in 2015, Rae contacted me and asked if I would write a blog for them, with new, or previously written material.

After a couple months, I finally wrote "Dick and Jane Go to Kindergarten," sharing my concerns about Common Core reading for kindergarteners. I went on to become a Featured Blogger for BAM. Already having more than fifty blogs on my personal *Reading Champs* website, and another eighty plus posted on BAM (not counting many left in draft, or completely lost by my ineptitude).

Hoping for an even wider audience, I decided to put together a collection of selected blogs, as essays, in hopes that each brief story of my life as teacher, mother, educator, and widow might inspire a reader, bring a tear or two, and hopefully encourage people to stand up in collective voice about making our world a better place. And because my life work is about the teaching of reading, as art and craft, I have included a number of 'how-to-teach-reading' articles as well.

Selecting, revising, and rewriting my stories took many months. Each one was so personal. Every piece offers something I believe to be very important in my life: questions I ponder, truths I hold dear, moments of sadness...and moments of joy. I hope each informs, motivates, and reaches you, dear reader, as they have me.

Teaching is a work of heart. Love and passion. The perfect go-togethers.

When all is said and done, life is about legacy. Each one of us shares a burning passion to do something, make a difference while we are here. In greatest humility, I am honored to share some of my stories. Maybe read a story or two a day, or perhaps straight through.

Here we go…

Leaving footprints on your reading hearts, Rita

Acknowledgments

I am basking in the light of love. It takes others to see what we might not see, or don't want to. Finding the truth is significant in celebrating my strong sense of purpose and legacy.

When others want us to be successful, there is no greater gift. I am truly blessed by such support.

Many people have been in the village of my life encouraging and helping me complete this book. To start with, thanking my family and friends, you'll meet some in my stories. Vicki, Shirley, Ellen, over the years, good friends mean a lot.

I have a large tight knit family, including my sister Sheryl and brother-in-law Rick. Also, Kristin, Heidi, Stephen, Danya, Jim and their kids. Five grandchildren. Nephews, nieces, Beth, Rita, Katrina, Steve, and Michael. Erinne and cousins, you are in my thought and heart.

To those angels watching over me, I know your light surrounds me. Remembering my parents who encouraged me to be a reader and teacher, plus husband William, brother Marshall, best friends, Pam Laird and Estelle Werve.

To Charles Palmer always supporting my writing.

To Don Werve for believing in this project, offering constant editorial ideas, assisting with revisions, proofreading and always encouraging me to finish.

To my Eugene little family: TJ, Rebecca and Morgan, my enduring gratitude. Thanks for suggesting ideas that made a difference, and always supporting me in my work. I recognize you sacrificed a lot of family time.

To Tom and Cheryl Thien, preschool directors. Thanks for mentoring me. Teaching young children brand new reading skills, such a joy.

To staff of Bell Avenue School. You guys made dreams come true and years later what we did shines brightly. Jeanette Kajka and Paula Weiss, special thanks for keeping me connected.

To Rebecca Hogue, of LifeRich for encouraging me. LifeRich Consultant Peter Parcon for answering so many questions and thanks also to my Lavidge publicist Courtney Vasquez.

To Errol St. Clair Smith, founder of BAM Internet Radio, for recognizing and supporting my work as a Featured writer.

To Sam Linhardt for suggesting I share my blogs with a larger audience, listening to my ideas, cheering me on when I was too tired to think, and believing there are no limits.

To Robin Tappan for time, expertise and belief in the book, offering production-ready, high-quality technical support, formatting, and editing, being an exceptional listener and creative presence.

To Hal Powers, author for listening and coaching me about my unique writing style and helping me polish art and craft.

To all the schools, children, parents, educators I met along the way, it's hard to believe I am still here, doing 'my thing' after forty-seven years. You made it possible.

To Giri Kowalke for friendship and technical help. Perfect having your neighbor be a techie.

To my life coach, Ava, thanks for keeping me grounded and trusting my capabilities.

Although a totally consuming project, so many people urged me toward the finish line it is impossible to list everyone here, but know I appreciate everyone's contributions.

Overcoming great obstacles, I compiled my stories about education, equity and fairness, love, life, family and friends, reading and literacy. Things we most care about.

Thank you for reading about my life. It means so much to me that I could do this. Last year I could barely think to put two sentences together. It seems like such a miracle.

Sometimes it takes just a word or two to change a life, or maybe validate your thoughts. I fervently hope my words have the power of belief, magic of unicorns, and the beauty of rainbows.

Leaving footprints on your reading hearts, Rita

INTRODUCTION

For my daughter, Rebecca: We did it!

In *Stories from a Teacher's Heart,* you'll find eight chapters of short stories that I selected to inform, validate your thinking, and hopefully inspire you to find or live your passion. At least, that's my intention.

These stories, originally written as blog posts, celebrate my journey from the mountains of northern California to Oregon's Willamette Valley. Along the way I watched the world swirl by me. My life changed from caring for my husband Bill, in the solitude of a historic home on mountain property, to starting over in a vibrant university community.

I find it almost impossible to believe that I am still a widow, seven years and four moves later. But there are mostly happy tears and laughs.

I write a lot about optimism and overcoming obstacles. I have been doing so for many years, not just now. I am always interested in what makes a champion, notably in literacy and life.

The winds of change wreaked havoc on my life and it has taken me quite awhile to right the ship and figure out which port I am sailing to. Just when my life was becoming settled in Oregon, I got the dreaded diagnosis. But that was later—earlier, I was just surviving, grieving, and moving. A champion never gives up. I came close.

During the journey I met love, experienced love, lost love, hurt and was hurt. My family and teaching sustained me. In my life, family and teaching always bring me back to my higher self.

Always writing about things that call to my heart or interest me, you will notice a thread weaving these missives together. So much has happened in my life and in the larger world, both good and not so, during the last few years. Lots of motivation for me to pick up my laptop and pour my heart out.

And so I did. Charlottesville. Transgender issues. School-to-prison pipeline. Equity. Testing. Kindergarten suspensions, etc. Tenacity keeps me going. I can't begin to write everything I'd like to. So what's here is specially selected and edited for you, with such gratitude.

My stories are stories we can all relate to. They are our shared, common bonds.

Perhaps start with a title that pops out to you. Chapter descriptions are included in the table of contents and are repeated at the beginning of each chapter. Story dates help put topics in context. Unfortunately, I had to leave out a lot of great stories when I edited the original manuscript for length, so sequences may be a little out of sync, but it won't matter.

Clearly the seasons of life and their inevitable transitions are relatable to all. Leadership, finding and living purpose and passion are also part of the human condition. I hope that my efforts inspire you to excellence. I also hope my words make you laugh, cry, forgive, forget, remember, savor, share…and love.

What in the world do lemonade stands, play, sleepovers and speed reading hacks have to do with each other? Everything! In my world, as mother and teacher-activist, it all blends into a glorious recipe for a purposeful life, filled with joy and love! You'll see.

Let's take a Book Walk and get you started.

Leaving footprints on your reading hearts, Rita

CONTENTS

CHAPTER 1
FAMILY LIFE, MAKING MEMORIES

A Teacher's Family Comes First: Meet the Family.

Chapter one introduces some of my large, extended family. I share my love and a bit of my life as a widow. Stories include Labor Day glamour camping and a hint of a love interest, lemonade stands as a rite of passage, graduations and family reunions. I loved writing "Sensei," about karate classes and empowerment. I happen to live really close to my Eugene kids, so there are several stories about being housebound during a blizzard, my granddaughter sleeping over, etc.

CHAPTER 2
LIFE TRANSITIONS: CHANGE INEVITABLE, GROWTH OPTIONAL

Teacher as a Survivor: Life Transitions, Change and Growth.

Chapter two reveals my thoughts and feelings about moving, overcoming fear, surviving cancer, and spreading grace through legacy. Career stages and life transitions highlight this sweet chapter filled with hopes and dreams and longing, as well as the realities of daily life. These are some of my favorite titles because I bared my soul.

CHAPTER 3
LEADERSHIP AND SOCIAL CONSCIENCE

Teacher as a Leader: Leadership and Social Conscience.

Chapter three is about strength, standing up for beliefs and sharing a collective voice for what we need to accomplish in our community, country, and world. I am a risk-taker by nature and speak out for justice and equity. As an educational activist, there were many stories I wanted to write, and some I simply couldn't bear to write. I did manage to put pen to paper, so to speak, on a number of major social issues that I found deeply disturbing or significant, like school shootings, DACA, Charlottesville, bullies and Title IX, the school-to-prison pipeline, equity through inclusion, and more.

CHAPTER 4
READING: THE GREAT DEBATE CONTINUES

Teacher as a Researcher: Celebrate My Passion, Reading.

Chapter four is not only informative, but also offers compelling rationale why we need to promote reading without tests. These collected stories suggest reasons to end the great, unending debate on how to teach reading and offer practical strategies for anyone teaching or coaching reading. You can practice speed-reading hacks, enjoy summer reading ideas for family fun, and find out how to appreciate the classics at home. I have included a couple interesting articles about boosting reading fluency, not retaining third grade challenged-readers, and the problem with too-early kindergarten reading instruction.

CHAPTER 5
LITERACY FOR ALL. WHY NOT?

Teacher as a Literacy Champion: Do Kids Have Right to Literacy?

Chapter five extends my essays about reading to the broader topic of 'literacy.' Reading and literacy are not interchangeable, as you find out. Important topics include banned books, world literacy day, right to literacy, national reading test scores and ready–to-use reading recipes for every teacher, parent or coach. Celebrate literacy with 'Read across America.' Get on your party hat! This chapter really packs a wallop.

CHAPTER 6
PRESCHOOL, TEACHING LITTLEST LEARNERS

Teacher as a Lifelong Learner: Making a Case for Universal Preschool.

Chapter six is sure to bring a smile to your face and a joyous moment or two in every missive. Everybody is a teacher, one way or another. But not everyone can be a great preschool teacher. I surely found that out! Enjoy my preschool adventures. Chapters one-through-four tell you quite a bit about me, but the sweet stories in this chapter reveal my growth as a teacher of youngest children. Preschool, for me, is a world of tiny kiddos learning emergent reading skills, during busy days filled with washing hands, outdoor play, sharing, and caring.

CHAPTER 7
DREAM THE DREAM, LIVING A LIFE OF PURPOSE

Teacher Modeling Empathy: Living a Life of Purpose.

Chapter seven, small but mighty, highlights my life as a servant leader—as well as follower. I have always known my purpose was to teach. I believe that along the way I have reached a lot of kids and adults. I know I keep learning and growing. Maintaining my humility has been easy these last years, as I have been sorely tested. In this moment, Lessons from Geese stands out because I hear geese honking overhead! As our world grows ever-closer, I pray we learn from each other and celebrate goodness, diversity and beauty. Several of my stories share commonalities, stunning views of everyday life, and strengthen our resolve as citizens of the world.

CHAPTER 8
THE SCHOOLHOUSE, AND LIFE'S REAL LESSONS

Teacher as a Thought Leader: School and Life Lessons.

Chapter eight treats you with pendulum-swinging hot topics. Explore my thoughts on homework, ditching textbooks, kindergarten suspensions, cursive writing, competition, and more. The home-to-school connection should be seamless and strong. Parents are in partnership with schoolhouses and have a lot to say about how things go down. This chapter makes connections about stuff that matters, from the home to the schoolhouse. Start thinking.

CHAPTER 1

FAMILY LIFE, MAKING MEMORIES
Teacher's Family Comes First: Meet the Family.

Chapter one introduces some of my large, extended family. I share my love and a bit of my life as a widow. Stories include Labor Day glamour camping and a hint of a love interest, lemonade stands as a rite of passage, graduations and family reunions. I loved writing "Sensei," about karate classes and empowerment. I happen to live really close to my Eugene kids, so there are several stories about being housebound during a blizzard, my granddaughter sleeping over, etc.

A) Family Glamping: A Lesson in Love
B) Lemonade Stands: Rule Breakers or Kid Makers?
C) Miss You! Family Grad Reunion
D) Sensei!
E) Morgan Sleeps Over! Seven Lessons I learned
F) Blizzard! Home Is Where the Heart Is
G) The Parrot, a Thanksgiving Parable
H) Congrats, Grads! Oh, the Places You'll Go!
I) Pennies from Heaven

1A

FAMILY GLAMPING: A LESSON IN LOVE
September 3, 2018

Labor Day, priorities and summer bliss.

I had an extraordinary day yesterday. Did you? And I can hardly wait to tell you what happened. I had so much fun with my family! I got my priorities straight; family first!

Here in America, the Labor Day holiday weekend is an end-of-summer opportunity to reflect and make observations about past and future. Lessons always surround us when we watch, listen, and learn. That proved to be so true for me yesterday.

We go through phases and stages in life where it seems like stuff is just rolling downhill faster than we can keep up. So I needed a break. A pause to savor life's beauties, feel the joys of each moment, and relish my 'happy.' I spent most of the summer getting healthy and figuring out the next phase in my life, post cancer. I also had some heartache and disappointments; don't we all?

A time of mindfulness, dance, watching sunsets and listening to rapids. A summer of promises made- some met, some not, some hurt, some joy. Best ever, notably the day I learned I am finally cancer free, with unmet life yet to be fulfilled. I'm still here, giving new promise to my legacy. Let's start with a lesson in family love.

What a super duper campsite.

My kids created a special end-of-summer family weekend. It was tough to plan for camping with unexpected road closures, questionable day-to-day air quality from various wildfires, and restricted burning, which meant no marshmallow campfires (overcome by a last minute switch to propane).

My son-in-law and daughter, always crafty and best planners ever, overcame all obstacles presented. And pulled off a magical family 'Glamping' (glamour camping) experience.

I just didn't want to go for three days when I had so much to do, so I volunteered to dog-sit Charlie, their little Griffonshire who looks like a Gremlin. I never missed a family holiday weekend outing before, and my kids were upset. Morgan was devastated. Morgan, now seven, is about to start school. How could I miss what were sure to be magical camping 'aha' moments? Family first. A lesson in love and perspective, what's important.

So yesterday, Sunday, spontaneous for me, I packed up a couple towels, made a picnic lunch, grabbed a guy friend to go for the fun. Grand idea!

The 'glamper' camp scene, very Griswoldian, but not really, was so awesome! Without campfire permitted, TJ and Rebecca set up the campsite complete with disc golf, games, cooking stoves, etc.

Daddy made up a new tackle box for Morgan's fishing equipment, and had already replaced her Barbie fishing pole with a big girl one, purple, of course.

Before the trip, TJ and I shopped with Morgan and picked up a very cool, comfy inflatable bed and set-ups for their oversize family tent. I could have fit in, but nah, kind of feh category for sleeping bags these days, but for the day-pass visit, tent life yesterday was heck of fun!

The campground was sheer wonder for Morgan. She got to fish with Mom and Dad, watch horseshoe games, BBQ and roast marshmallows, made a new friend, played pool in the clubhouse.

Back to the tent. Imagine a big one, with floor covered with matting, loads of sleeping bags, pillows and blankets on large air beds. Glamping at its finest! Morgan brought her Baby Alive Doll, small dolls, Barbies, couple of Kens, a new Jo Jo doll, usual hair bows, books, her Kindle. Everything fit into the little monogrammed pink suitcase I gave her a couple years ago, when she was still little.

I heard Morgan was waking up about 5 a.m., so it's a good thing I wasn't sleeping there. Plus I have really obnoxious insomnia. Morgan will tell you she definitely doesn't believe in napping, so that's not happening. Kid code.

But there were a couple of really big life lessons destined to be for me, which I'm sharing with you now. Let's go back to the beginning of the day trip.

Granddaughter power and the strength of family.

I didn't know how it would go, just a hunch it would be ok to bring a possible new suitor. My kids said yes. I had to trust my instincts that it would be fine. A lesson in love.

When she first saw me arrive, my granddaughter yelled "Nana"! I knew it was a good thing I made the effort to visit. Then she met my friend and called out, "Keep him, Nana," and hung on him like her new best friend. I couldn't believe it.

A game of pool was first thing on Peanut's agenda. I was not into horseshoes as I got hit by one when I was a kid. I always got in the big kids' way. Morgan is a hustler. She learned to play pool this summer at the Boys' and Girls' Club. Between us, I'm not sure who was the worst player. It didn't matter. I'm so non-competitive.

Then Morgan took me aside and told me, "Don't mess it up," although I wasn't quite sure what our seven-year-old counselor meant. In the clubhouse she turned on the little old TV, pulled a chair over, told me to sit, and proceeded to talk with my friend about me. I heard her tell him I spill all over myself (true), I need naps (true), I am tired all the time (right, Barbies get exhausting), and that I snore (also true, maybe a snort, too).

And more. Morgan told my friend how to set up a fancy date night with me, how I act and that I am lonely. That was a corker. So I had to move us to the campsite into safer territory, or so I thought. Life lesson in love, taught by a seven-year-old. She said, "He's a keeper, Nana!"

Back at the campsite, comfy, playing with dolls, dramatic play amidst the beautiful natural lake environment. Morgan gave her love freely, shared her three-day camping experience, taught us how to be in nature, as she knows it, offered gigantic smiles, told stories of a new little girl friend, ate s'mores, and slept in a big tent with Mommy and Daddy.

By late afternoon, I was indeed content. Joining my family for a magical outdoor experience in its simplest form was the right idea after all. I had to trust my instincts, since I am no longer into camping that much. I prefer the comforts of home. So, of course as it got stuffy and warmer in that tent, I was ready for a little snooze; not to be had.

Camping anywhere, backyard, in nature, in a den or bedroom is such a grand way for families to turn off electronics and reconnect with one another. However, nothing beats Mother Nature.

Outdoor camping meant figuring out which critter got into the tent to nibble and leave crumbs and messes. Share often told campfire stories, eat hot dogs and chips, maybe cookies, not just gluten free. Experiencing the campground showers, miniature golf, disc golf, such simple pleasures! That's what my family got to enjoy this weekend.

Families always come first. Together time, like the way it used to be. Before life got so hectic and unsteady, families sharing a quiet time of mindfulness. By listening to breezes, singing old long forgotten camp songs, families transition from one season to the next, sharing a lesson in love, trust, and bonding.

As school bells ring, hoping your last summer adventures, on the lake, in the library, at a campsite, carry happy thoughts and simple pleasures throughout your days of many blessings. Sending family, schoolhouse and workplace love, from my heart to yours.

Leaving footprints on your reading hearts, Rita

1B

LEMONADE STANDS: RULE BREAKERS OR KID MAKERS?

August 11, 2018

Childhood is a precious time, what's the rush?

As summer draws to a close and back-to-school bells ring, families enjoy the tail end of summer bliss. Popsicle sticks and lemonade stands. Kids everywhere making lemonade, at least I think so.

When I think of my childhood summers, such vivid memories of long days playing with neighbor kids, trips to Lake Michigan with my family, going fishing and planting pansies with my Dad.

I spent time with my Mom reading, viewing old movies, playing Scrabble and watching her do crossword puzzles.

In order to get money for cherry cokes down at the corner and maybe save for new shoe skates, or even go horseback riding, we had a lot of lemonade stands. It was no big deal. It was a rite of passage, a part of summer like eating watermelon, chomping on sweet corn on the cob and picking berries.

Long, leisurely summer days reading books and going to the library. Taking the bus by ourselves, to downtown and back.

Lemonade stands were most fun of all. We earned our own money and that was a very big deal.

All my friends had lemonade stands. Everybody did it. All summer long, sometimes in the fall and spring, too. We always talked about hot chocolate stands in the winter, but never did it. We had our stands set up on the lawn or drive. Our parents were home. A lot of learning and bonding went on.

Before long, babysitting took over my financial life, which meant layaways at local department store. What a cool thing to finally pay off the clothes and take them home. But I'm not sure that lemonade stand came first, showed us how to do it. Make money, have fun, help others, share and gain confidence. Big gains, even if little or no profit, really.

Recently 'Education Week' had an article about lemonade stands and entrepreneurship. It seems like it all fits together, doesn't it? Our seven year old had a lemonade stand a couple weeks ago.

It turned out to be a not great weekend, extremely hot and county fair weekend, but Peanut still netted about $20.00. She even split $6.00 with her morning shift lemonade partner. I think about $20.00 total went into her piggy bank. But I'm not sure since Daddy paid for product and cups. I got three free glasses.

My point is, we are not talking about big business here. Far from it. I have no idea how much the average home driveway, lawn or corner lemonade stand brings in, but I bet not much. Probably just using a big box or table, chair, couple signs but it may be an elaborate dramatic play pre-made stand, there goes the profit even further. What profit?

Peanut learned about health and safety, promoting her lemonade project, making change and sales. "Get your cold lemonade here!" She said selling was her favorite part. I also observed her sharing and having fun, making signs with her friend for a couple hours in the morning. She gave her $3.00, as I said, but that was pretty much all her profit to that point. Pricing, perfect. One cup, $1.00, two cups, $2.00. Can't beat that for competitive pricing.

It's maybe a matter of perspective. And some really crazy stuff, at least to me, has been happening to kids with their lemonade stands. Permits? Health and Safety Codes? Is it Legal? Taxable income?

I never thought I'd be writing about kids and lemonade stands. Not in a million years, so to speak. But here we are. This is quite a non-issue issue for everybody to think about. Maybe you already have an opinion, one way or another. Did you ever have a lemonade stand? Or your children?

I read an interesting article forwarded by a mama interested in what's happening to children's lemonade stands, meaning being shut down. It happened to her kids. There is even a petition circulating around the country, allowing lemonade stands, so it's not just a local question anymore. Permits, fees, health inspections, it's just too much to contemplate.

Harsh lessons in overzealous regulations have shut down lemonade stands in Colorado, Oregon, and other states, with laws being proposed to exempt child businesses of temporary nature such as lemonade stands.

Imagine having to seek out and obtain food service establishment permits, health permits, business permits, legal permits and vending licenses, etc. just to re-live the simple childhood pleasure of the 1950's, the lemonade stand.

Moreover, many kids and organizations hold lemonade stands to benefit children's charities such as children with cancer, immigrant groups, church and local projects, etc. Way more benefits than just feeding a piggy bank, in a lot of instances.

So a neighbor calls and complains, that's enough to bring out the police, acting upon that complaint and voila! A non-issue of any real bones is now a legal one and a stand is shut down. Kaput. Fines. Or, knowing that these permits must be in hand, hundreds of dollars potentially could be charged up front for a stand netting little to nothing.

Assuming cookies are packaged and lemonade safely juiced and properly handled, I see no big deal about the time-tested lemonade stand.

I don't think safety is the main concern. I think it's the location. Personally I wonder if it's that kids have moved their tables or stands to art festivals, fairs or other more commercial spots, or environs which makes it look competitive. If a lot of money is being made, is it interfering with bigger businesses? But I really don't know.

Do people really believe lemonade buyers do it for the excellence of the drink? Does this supplant buying a coke or a beer? I think not. Ridiculous. But unless kids today have permits and laws are changed to end this cacophony of harassment in the name of civic duty, I would think twice before planning and putting up a stand other than on lawn or drive. And definitely know local laws.

Not much time for spontaneity, this needs a lot more thinking and planning. Maybe a good idea to review our state laws regarding the subject. Maybe a better idea to get involved, as the Colorado mama did, to effect change on behalf of her kids and other kids.

I always say childhood is a precious time. What's the rush? Summer offers a chance to enjoy being kids with our kids, reading grand stories and most certainly doing a lemonade stand or two. Let kids be kids! How about a glass of lemonade right now? Yum!

Leaving footprints on your reading hearts, Rita

1C

Miss You! Family Grad Reunion
June 17, 2017

It seems these days that families live so far apart. I'm sure that's the way it is for most of us. Keeping connected takes a lot more effort than it used to. I don't think it is just my large family.

Screen sharing is not the same as being together in real time, although it somewhat fills the gaps.

I feel like a slacker. Lately I've been losing things, including house keys and my wallet, twice. Moving much too fast. Not exactly self-care. I finished helping at the preschool until September and the preschool was the first graduation. We had seven children graduating and what a fun, imaginative production for all the children.

It seems like I've been on a treadmill lately, such a busy time of year. I looked forward to going up to Beaverton to take a much needed family-filled break.

First night I made it through ok, then back to my typical self, at breakfast, the day of the festivities, I smashed my hand in the dishwasher, imagine that, and was icing during the graduation ceremony I missed.

Honestly, I've been behind on most birthdays and special events ever since I moved to Eugene. While I lived in the California mountains with my husband William, our large extended family joined us at our historic home and property. When I finally moved to Eugene to be with one of our kids, it felt like splinters of our solid old wood house.

There comes a time in our life when we stop looking through the rearview mirror, focusing on the now, hoping and planning for the future. Sometimes it's easier to live through our memories, which truth be told, may be somewhat tainted in recollection, the ways things were supposed to be, rather than how they were.

Graduations and Reunions go together, don't you agree? A time to reflect, hold one another tight, maybe even make needed amends for some long past infraction, perhaps one you weren't even aware of. If only everyone could attend, but for those who make it, how glorious.

This time together had special meaning for me, spending time with my sister, Sheryl, catching up with grown up 'kids' I hadn't seen for a long time, who I held in my arms as babies. There are so many other family members I hope to visit this year. I'm so overdue.

We had several graduates this year. The Beaverton weekend grads included kindergarten, eighth and high school. And several loose front teeth.

Who's Who, Cast of Characters: Sarah's high school graduation.

Every time I visited our Beaverton, Oregon family, it was filled with athletics, one game after another, baseball, my favorite. Last year Jacob graduated, a fine student, athlete and young man. Now it was Sarah's turn. Almost empty nesters, I think Mom and Dad will be just fine, relieved of all the games, coaching and school functions. However, two out of state tuitions leave me breathless.

Sarah was outstanding in school, playing five varsity sports, water polo, racquetball, softball, swim team and track and field. She advanced to districts for javelin and discus and made it to the podium. Sarah who was so liked she was also school Princess, will be attending Cal Poly, San Luis Obispo in the fall, studying engineering.

About eighty friends attended the home party. Adding in the family, of course, so there were about one hundred people, all over the place. What a fun celebration. Laughed, I didn't even get a cupcake, at the time, but later I ended up eating one, courtesy of Sarah.

Precocious eight year old, Emily still at home. Just lost another tooth. So much was going on, she said "Aunt Rita, tooth fairy forgot me." I told her it was because of the bed hopping, with company there, tooth fairy wasn't sure what bed she was in." Mom took care of it the next night. Said she completely forgot.

Brendon and his parents, Mike and Katrina flew from Europe; Brendon had been studying French. Berkeley student, a term abroad was amazing for him and we laughed together about our mutual dislike of cheese, except pizza, of course, and how he survived all the cheese. He grew out his hair, very curly and looks so 70's. I remember playing Legos with him and now he has a double major in sciences and French. Very smart and charming.

We watched the old classic movie "Weird Science" with some of the older kids and laughed so hard.

Adam graduated eighth grade, in Temecula, California. Unimaginable. Where did the years go? Mastered martial arts and now studying piano, Adam hung out with adults and the two littlest, all weekend. What a sweetheart. Going into high school. Always an artist, and very bright, Adam is such a joy to be around. I had missed him so.

I went to the Reunion with my daughter Rebecca, husband, TJ and Morgan. Fairly short Griswold road trip, but still heard, "Are we almost there yet?" after the first half hour, and had to stop at Subway, gluten free buns. Morgan is graduating from Kindergarten next week in Eugene. She lucked out and not only was in a brand new tech-based school, her Kindergarten teacher rocked it.

All together in spirit.

I just wish all the rest of our extended family could have been with us. Life splinters us so. However, other plans are in the works for get-togethers.

Morgan is coming for another sleepover this weekend. I have some ideas of things to do, special for her Kindergarten graduation, because I need to be in California with my sister and have to miss. It's two weeks late, also, because of all the weather days.

Jacob came home for a quick trip after his freshman year at college in Washington State. He towers over me now. I remember him as a baby. Fortunately he stayed with his friend a couple nights, checking in and out, so I got a bed. The first night I was on futon detail with my daughter, Rebecca. She said I snored. Probably did.

Morgan, six, was in bliss with her cousin Emily, age eight. They are our youngest now, but growing up so fast!

We have two Rita's in our family. My nephew Steve chose wisely. Rita and Steve pulled together the massive home party, and radiated joy and love of family. Offering their home to so many grads and family members. How do you spell love?

Steve made an outstanding slide show of our family, featuring the kids growing up, so many memories. I think I watched it more than a couple times straight through, everyone was in it, past and present, quite a production. Shed more than a few tears.

My sister Sheryl and husband Rick were with us, so very important to me. They live in California, so now I don't see them very often. Our love is deep and I miss them so.

Uncle Willy flew in from San Francisco. I talked a little politics with him, not much, politics being a taboo topic this weekend, and no news was watched. A good thing, probably.

Rita's Mom and Dad flew in from southern California, as well, so it was really neat to see that part of the family. Jessica, another family member lives in Beaverton, too, so I got to catch up with her life.

My niece Beth couldn't attend, she was stuck in NYC with flu. It was a sorely missed piece of our family pie.

If you ever want to see diversity, a family who gets along, resolves issues that may come up, ours is a great example.

This grad Reunion was one only one part of our wonderful family. We have a maternal side, paternal side, various cousins, nephews, nieces and I really need to do a Family Tree; there are so many shoots and branches and twigs off branches, not to mention TJ's family, also quite extensive.

Who we were.

- We represent varying political philosophies. Yet we respect our opinions.
- We are of different nationalities and consider that a plus.
- We are of several religions, explore and share each.
- We take care of each other with love and empathy.
- We are Americans and proud to be Americans.

In our turbulent times, the institutions of graduations, including the protocol and rituals offer a continuation of life that we count on.

Rites of passage.

Graduations, with or without a family reunion, are rites of passage, a cause of celebration, in the rich tradition of yesterday and the bright promise of tomorrow.

Tonight I count my blessings I had opportunity to share another special event in my life, tearfully regret my husband was not there with us, but savor the experience of celebratory bliss.

To all grads, families, friends and loved ones, I send you peace and harmony tonight, a wish for peace in our hearts, nation and world.

Leaving footprints on your reading hearts, Rita

1D

SENSEI!

May 21, 2017

Champions in school, champions at life. Respect.

Thank you to our Sensei, master teacher for teaching us never-ending, continual improvement. "Kai Zen!"

Karate classes, taught by Sensei, extraordinary meshing of kids and Instructor.

Listen to the children with me, powering up their spirits with the sound of "Kiai!" (sounds like "kee-eye"). Here we go! Outfits on, belts tied, spirits soaring.

Saying no to bullies.

More than that. Ready to enhance balance, build muscle tone, follow directions and master martial arts skills. Watching the kids train, I also notice an unexpected benefit of hand-eye coordination which is a valuable reading skill. I never thought I would see a reading benefit from karate.

Any mention of Karate always reminds me of the classic Karate Kid movies. You know the ones I mean. First and best will always be the original 1984 "Karate Kid," starring Pat Morita and Ralph Macchio. Recall the new kid in town tormented by bullies, until he is taken under wing by karate master, a humble gardener, Mr. Miyagi. Unforgettable.

The idea of Sensei is so strong, as we recall vivid images of the wise man instructing the adolescent boy through unexpected training in mindfulness, painting fences, washing cars, preparation for eventual learning martial arts and life skills. Happy endings.

I see our students playing Ninja on varied playground equipment, and Ninja teachers are definitely out there. Too many Ninja Turtles tee shirts to count this year. But this is not the same as the true Sensei.

I believe most teachers are Sensei, in terms of honor, respect, builders of confidence, instructors of skills. In its truest sense, Sensei teachers may have been teaching a long time gaining great wisdom, art and craft. But time is not necessarily the defining factor.

Sensei is in all of us.

There's no time table in becoming Sensei, although it's said to mean 'one before another' and usually refers to a venerable person, greatly experienced in the art.

My Eugene granddaughter, Morgan, continues to surprise me with her age-six interests. We've been through classes of gymnastics and ballet. Morgan would like to play soccer, but in Eugene, since children are so used to the rain, their games are outside and Morgan can't do that, another story sometime.

Morgan kept asking about Karate. It's not just for boys. Then she found a new home. In her class there are four little boys and she's the only girl, which makes it pretty cool. She likes it. She's barely started, but I saw a big difference in only a few sessions.

Morgan's Sensei, just like you.

Here's what I notice in Karate class:

1. Consistent routines, beginning, middle, end of class.
2. Transitions connecting prior and new learning.

3. Checks for understanding continually.
4. Teaches basic Japanese vocabulary through immersion. (Includes greetings, commands, counting to ten, open and close class.)
5. Inspires children to excellence, motivates, builds confidence.
6. Creates a culture of learning and constant growth.

Benefits for Morgan's class:

1. Mental, physical, emotional connections.
2. Learn to focus, concentrate, take turns.
3. Balance. Poses and activities enhance balance.
4. Mindfulness with Intention. Patience.
5. Following rules and commands.
6. Speaking basic Japanese phrases.
7. Exercise and agility training.
8. Develop a sense of accomplishment.

I love watching Sensei Elida working with the children. With great respect shown, preschool and kinders are already getting ready for their first recital at the beginning of June. They practice being in front of an audience, being judged on correctness of moves, which determines their new level and color of belt.

Morgan gets dressed at home, ready for immediate action. I missed the last class and was surprised to see a video of the kids sparring. Morgan looks like she is holding her own, with a bigger, more experienced boy. She knows she is strong, coordinated and determined to master karate now.

Having Karate goals for Life.

Morgan is eager to tell about the various belts and describe what she has to know, and how to do it right to get those belts. Having goals set, practicing at home and bragging rights with the boys at school. Nice.

Yes, girls learn Karate, too.

I heard the Kindergarteners, at least the boys, didn't believe Morgan was in Karate, that's for boys. When my daughter Rebecca went to read to the class, she said, "Yes, Morgan is absolutely in Karate." After all, girls can do whatever they set out to do. And that is quite a life lesson.

I like the idea of calling our nation's teachers, Sensei. There is such dedication, so much love.

Morgan now knows how to break out of any grab hold and her Mom told me self-protection is an added benefit of the Karate training. No bullies better get near Morgan now.

As a lefty, I wasn't sure whether this would impede any of her movements, but so far fine, and as I mentioned, the hand-eye coordination is really helpful.

I am pretty certain Morgan will continue Karate, at least for a while, and these skills and attitudes will always be part of her life.

Her classroom teacher is a Sensei too, so this Kindergarten year has been a great one for Morgan. When I sit watching the karate classes I see an amazing Sensei, and happy kids engaged and in flow state.

"Owadi-masu." Let's end class now.

I hope the young children I teach every day see me as Sensei. At least I know I am giving it my all. "Kiai!"

Leaving footprints on your reading hearts, Rita

1E

MORGAN SLEEPS OVER! SEVEN LESSONS I LEARNED
April 8, 2017

Do you remember the first time you had a sleepover?

Along with that first loose tooth, this is one great big rite of passage.

Lately I find myself spending more time listening to the ever-present Eugene rain, Soundscapes and relaxation music. If I look at social media I get fixated on mindless, fun stuff or very inspirational real life stories and musings.

Except for the teaching, not much makes sense to me right now. I kind of feel like that scene in the movie "2012" where the North and South Poles switch places. Maybe I am sort of like the Woody Harrelson character, sure those secret ships will take us up and away.

I'm now a fan of therapy dogs Max and companion Ruby, Esther the Wonder Pig and cat videos—although I am allergic to cats. There are a lot of wonderful, kind-hearted people in this world. That's what I'm focusing on.

Lesson one: Children make everything worthwhile.

Still innocent awhile longer, we watch and feel the world through their eyes, ears and souls. Take time to savor the moment. Make it our intention, first and foremost. Prioritize and balance. Let our senses be filled with what our kiddos feel, hear, touch and taste, the newness of it, like that newborn giraffe on wobbly legs.

Lesson two: We had a big 'first' this weekend.

Morgan is growing up. She spent most of the weekend alone with me, this time no mommy or daddy, sleeping in the downstairs old-fashioned high brass bed. That's a really comforting room. It's filled with kid-friendly old school photos and extended family memories.

It was really safe being here with mommy. But being a grown up Kinder, just turned six, maybe just maybe she could let Mom and Dad have an actual birthday date night. Hang out with me, sleep in the loft with me. And so she did.

One of my favorite classic kids' books is *Ira Sleeps Over*, by Bernard Waber, 1972. I just love this book. Have you read it? It's a sweet story about the first sleep- over. Ira got really excited about going over to Reggie's house. But he had a problem. What do you think it is? He was afraid to bring his teddy bear and look like a baby. Life is reduced to simplest terms.

Of course there are life lessons all the way through this book, but the parallel with our Kinder was taking the leap, that first separation leap of faith.

Beyond birthday parties, sleepovers help our kiddos feel important, independent and show a little grit. Sleepovers teach organizing, sequencing, learning what to pack, folding, and trusting our friends or nanas. Everything will be ok.

Lesson three: Packing takes time.

A packing trial run was a necessity. I stopped by my kids' house on the way home from school to see if Morgan was ready for the weekend. She was already packing on Thursday, and had way more than Ira did for his sleep- over at Reggie's. He was pretty much set with PJs, a blankie, slippers, and finally: Tah dah! His teddy.

Morgan's packing, another story. One suitcase was completely filled with favorite Dr. Seuss books. She could barely lift it. We compromised on two titles I didn't have in my collection (which we never read).

Morgan's rolling 'Morgan' bag was stuffed with matching and non-matching outfits and assorted shoes, leggings, slippers, movie star worthy. Stuffies, dolls including Snackin' Sara, a play dough consumer, (giant Barbie stayed home), light up glow-in-dark turtle, stars on ceiling. Blankets. Troll pillow. A lot of stuff!

Lesson four: Plan a lot, expect to do nothing on your list.

I was so ready. Visit the Art gallery on University of Oregon campus? A movie? Miniature golfing? Science Factory? Library downtown? My list overflowed a piece of paper. I offered all the ideas to Morgan. Of course, she had her very own and a lot of secrets and surprises.

Lesson five: Remember Maslow. Basic needs to meet.

Dramatic Play was what she wanted to do, plus go to dinner for sushi. Morgan had her own ideas about most things, from snack to non-schedule I had set. She decided to come right back to my house. First she checked to see things were the same. She hadn't been here much lately. And of course, what I had to eat here.

I was mostly over at my Eugene kids' house this hard-core winter. So it was critical to do an overall house inspection for her things. Her towels were out, little stools in the bathrooms, tub toys, princess plate and cup.

What was missing was my giant poodle Gus, who went to heaven after the recent life-altering Eugene storm. Morgan had not wanted to be here without Gus, added to no mommy or daddy. So that was another hurdle. Sometimes there are no perfect explanations.

Lesson six: Be fully present. No technology.

Just one-on-one special time and memories being made, that's the real meaning of sleep over.

Dramatic play and a walk to the school around the corner recess yard for outdoor time when it stopped raining, just wondrous.

Morgan loves to spend time in what she calls her "office." A tiny nook I put together, it's loaded with a writing center in mini, craft supplies, favorite books, etc. I couldn't figure out where colored pencils and art items were disappearing, then they turned up in the piano bench she sits on.

Stashed the sheet music somewhere. Piano bench was suddenly filled with little teacher items, as chalk, pens, notepads, etc. Bossy Teacher game, which I truly detest, but so hilarious, in a way. Mirrored me at that age. Her teacher would laugh so hard, though. "No time-out for me," I said, "no way!"

On went my old ballerina outfit, then my Mom's high heels, my Kimono, my fancy long dresses from family weddings. Darling. Just like her mama did in her time as my little girl.

Lesson seven: Forget cooking at Nana's.

Dinner, sat at sushi bar watching the chefs, eating seaweed salad and safe for kiddos Japanese food. Breakfast out, her doll Snackin' Sarah came along, needed a booster seat, but no more highchair now. The doll ate play dough, a perfect eater. Mama love through a generation of Barbies, but this doll cracks me up.

After dinner, we put on the movie "Sing." Of course, exhausted I immediately fell asleep, cuddled up on the couch. About an hour past bedtime Morgan woke me saying, "Nana I want to go to bed." LOL.

And finally, bedtime.

Up in our loft, I adjusted the various lights and pillows, read *Goodnight Moon, Love You Forever* (tears of course), and snuggled with my little peanut.

With those little fingers grasping my hand, I finally heard the comforting breathing, sounding just like her mama did when she was little, but getting bigger so fast. And she slept.

Children are our legacy on angels' wings. Morgan can't wait for our next sleepover. She's coming this weekend.

Now we'll know how to pack. Now we'll know not to plan. Now we'll know to let Morgan do her thing, with structure, of course. I am planning a trip to the new nearby bead store. I'd like to do some bead stringing there and maybe a project here. But I'll have to let you know, after all, Morgan has her own ideas.

In this time of uncertainties we live in, let us all share the joy of our children of all ages, finding peace, relaxation, freedom from worry, spending our time loving one another and serving others.

It all starts with that leap of faith.

Leaving footprints on your reading hearts, Rita

1F

BLIZZARD! HOME IS WHERE THE HEART IS
January 8, 2017

Weathering the storms of life: I can't get home!

Maybe with a drone, certainly not even my trusty Subaru with a car seat, would venture out in this weather. Sheets of ice, some obvious, some hidden, lurking. Even walking like a penguin, I can't manage going out the door at the moment.

My big poodle slipped on the ice today, and so did several of our friends. So obviously it makes sense to just stay put, read a good book, hang out on Twitter. Luckier this time, power is on. Makes one appreciative when things are going ok.

Mother Nature unleashed her fury this winter in Eugene. Maybe where you are, too. Ice storms, freezing rain, snow and ice have pummeled us pretty much non-stop for weeks now. I've been staying with my kids most of this time because my pellet stove broke and my house is freezing. The heat system can't keep up with the cold.

And the power was out for five days. I drove to school in areas strewn with mangled, downed trees, smashed cars, trees on roof, you get the idea. Eugene? Unthinkable. When I moved here I expected a mild climate. I have a lot of umbrellas, couple raincoats. And layers.

Public school classes have been closed so much I'll bet school goes until end of June, maybe later. This is really tough on teachers to keep up the momentum.

Our school had four kids last week. I made it two days, then couldn't get there. Guilt ridden. Teacher Tom told me it wasn't safe to attempt it. Unimaginable, no 'littles.'

Being with Morgan is kinder joy, however, and memories in the making. She was bursting to get back to her school. One of seven in her class on Friday, PJ Day, a belated *Polar Express,* and hot cocoa. I picked her up, carefully navigating the parking lot ice.

Go figure. No matter how prepared I thought I was, sometimes things just happen. Weather. Life. How unpredictable. Weathering the storm.

I am home. Priorities.

- Home is where the heart is. And my heart is clearly here with my family.
- How fortunate power is on and we are cozy and warm.
- How fortunate we have food to eat. Stocked up ahead, and during a 'window.'
- How fortunate so far no more trees crashing down. Like the one that hit my house.
- How fortunate everyone is here together, safe today. Circle of love. A love fest.

Family engagement.

- Surrender and enjoy the 'staycation.'
- Family reading, board games, maybe a good movie.
- Listen to and talk with each other. With no distractions, enjoy the quiet time.

Provide updates.

- Extended family and friends want to know what's going on, and number one, ensure we are safe and warm.

- Putting up funny Facebook posts, as well as weather reports, brings out our fun side.
- Cell phone catch up and Face Time.

Party! Celebrate the good things.

1. PJs. Cocoa and popcorn.
2. Dance party is such a riot.
3. Twister. Shake your booty!
4. Snapchat. Love it.
5. Make time stand still, fun!
6. Laugh. Lots. Tell jokes and stories. Sing. Make up lyrics.
7. Ok, a little You Tube and Go Noodle.
8. Watch "The Crown" on Netflix.

What I learned.

- Get a shovel. It can snow in Eugene.
- Keep a good attitude. I cannot control this situation.
- Bring more novels and junk magazines.
- Napping A-OK. Take a break.
- Do Pilates. Meditate.
- Clean and do overdue projects.
- Look at old photos. Maybe sort and organize.

Funny stuff.

- Send cat videos via Direct Message on Facebook.
- More Snapchat.

Be fully present.

- This is my opportunity to model good decision making for my kids.

- Use this gift of time to spend quality heartwarming memories with Morgan.
- My chance to do nothing and clear my head.
- Celebrate the good in our life as a family. Share our gratitude.

Lesson planning.

- All the kids are due back at school Tuesday, so I have a few more days to rethink what worked last week and transition after so many weather days.
- If I can get there safely and mostly stress free, I will go.
- My creativity is in high gear. Writing mini lessons for emergent phonics, sight words and word family patterns, and geography.

'Life Lessons' for us all.

Having a positive attitude in all difficult situations and making the best possible choices in fractions of time, tests us. I know now that eventually life will thaw again, trails open up and flowers bloom. It's like that.

Each life season offers us opportunity to celebrate the positive, work on whatever we need to fix, then move beyond whatever stuck us to the past, even what wasn't working.

I knew, after living in the mountains with my husband for many years, to always have a secondary heat source. I was really angry with myself for a couple weeks I was stuck with a dud pellet stove, of all things.

Then I reframed it, and got it right. My other Eugene home was waiting for me, their fireplace is perfect, their hearts filled with love.

Leaving footprints on your reading hearts, Rita

1G

THE PARROT: A THANKSGIVING PARABLE.
November 22 2017

I hope you enjoy this story, perfect for your Thanksgiving festivities.

Traditionally my family has always shared stories, our thanks of course, made plenty of toasts, and I always wrote plays for the kids.

Once in awhile we found something really fun to share at the table; this one came to me a long time ago from a friend, then I sourced it to a book called "All Kinds of Humor," 2012. The author Dennis Clark wrote it in 1996. Maybe it's familiar to you, there were a couple variations. Anyway, here goes. Get your grin on, and maybe some life lesson may pop into your head.

The Parrot. Some gift!

A young man named John received a parrot as a gift. The parrot had a bad attitude and an even worse vocabulary. Every word out of the bird's mouth was rude, obnoxious and laced with profanity.

John tried and tried to change the bird's attitude by consistently saying only polite words, playing soft music and anything else he could think of to 'clean up' the bird's vocabulary.

Finally, John was fed up and yelled at the parrot. The parrot yelled back. John shook the parrot and the parrot got angrier and even ruder.

John, in desperation, threw up his hand, grabbed the bird and put him in the freezer. For a few minutes the parrot squawked and kicked and screamed. Then suddenly there was total quiet. Not a peep was heard for over a minute. Fearing that he'd hurt the parrot, John quickly opened the door to the freezer.

The parrot calmly stepped out onto John's outstretched arms and said "I believe I may have offended you with my rude language and actions. I'm sincerely remorseful for my inappropriate transgressions and I fully intend to do everything I can to correct my rude and unforgivable behavior."

John was stunned at the change in the bird's attitude. As he was about to ask the parrot what had made such a dramatic change in his behavior, the bird continued,

"May I ask what the turkey did?"

I can think of a number of occasions this story has parallels, and infinite considerations. What might John have done differently? How do we change our attitudes and corresponding actions?

As you celebrate this joyous Thanksgiving, I send you my love, and of course gratitude. Gratitude for all you do to make this world a better, more wonderful place. We are one, turkeys and parrots all together.

God bless you all,

Leaving footprints on your reading hearts, Rita

1H

Congrats, Grads! Oh, the Places You'll Go!
June 18, 2016

Never give up! There is no failure, only feedback.

Question to our sweet little grad. "What was your favorite thing about graduating preschool last Sunday?"

Answer: "Wearing the white outfit with the funny hat."

Well, that about sums it up. The bigger kids getting set for big kids' school. The little kids also wearing caps and gowns because they were jealous, and graduated to pre-kindergarten. A grand performance including dancing, singing, little speeches by each child standing on a platform, and of course my favorite part, the pledge of allegiance.

Teachers gave every child a personalized book and each family a unique keepsake gift made by their child. Virtuosity of teacher love and amazing student performances. Laughter, tears of joy. Oh, the places these children will go! I'm so sure of that. Childhood is a precious time!

I am so happy to write this graduation post and admittedly nervous. The last time I was this jittery was right before I gave a Commencement speech for Chapman University. I practically fell off the platform. Tripped, no kidding, but I think I made up for it with what I said. My three best words were, "Just Do It."

We're closing in on the end of grad season, so today's the day I share my thoughts, hopefully motivate, inspire, and thank you for a great learning year. We had four grads in our family this season, one to go. That's what makes it dicey, to get to them all, preschool through high school. The family reunion part is the best and seeing in my head that little kid now all grown up, towering over me. I am the shrimp in the family, no longer the baby, but 'Nana' of the babies.

Lately I've been sorting stacks of photos, probably like you at this joyful time in life, and am amazed how time flew, my kids now grown up with their kids, and a lot of graduating. The life cycle continues. The rituals and celebrations matter enormously.

I think of each family graduate, the games we attended, the tears, the prom dates or lack of, school projects, curfews and messy rooms. Now my kids tell me all the not great things they pulled off we didn't know about. They say my husband and I were the strictest parents of all. Probably because I was a Principal and Bill had been the kid who was too cool for words.

Once I was called by the high school, that my daughter cut class. I said to give her detention for forging the note. I was pretty rough on her. She ended up being in the *Breakfast Club* for a month. When she graduated high school, then college, I knew we had done a darn good job raising her. Our four kids their special graduations. Now their kids are graduating.

Graduations are an important part of the life cycle. Not only do we celebrate our children's successes, we hold our collective breath, what's next? Lately I've been reading that most graduation speeches this year focused on overcoming adversity, technology and the global aspect of our life. Keynotes also highlighted the tragic, the need for inclusion. Equity. And I am not sure, but I think an end to violence. Wouldn't that be wondrous?

I have faith in our graduates. I have faith in our country. I believe each of our children is ready to take on the world. I know that our nation's teachers are extraordinary and I commend Principals for being role models setting the tone, offering vision and making sure each child graduates with skills necessary for success in today's fast paced world. The future is now.

How do we send off our children in the very best way? Pebbles to stumble over, mountains to climb. Hope. Passion.

I just love graduations of every kind and find reasons to routinely celebrate. I felt I graduated when I sent off my first Tweet last year on Twitter. I am such a lifelong learner. That's what we want for our kids. It's the way to life success, constant learning. There is so much more to know in our too rapidly changing data-driven world.

At the moment, I'm hanging out in the middle of a beehive of family activity. A few minutes ago, newly five dressed up for her Daddy and gave a rousing performance. I dug out two of my well-used classroom microphone sets: the old box kind, with wireless mikes. It was very old-fashioned, low technology, but not to Morgan.

I'm living in the moment when I'm with my family. Newly five is now outside in her party dress batting at a baseball, waiting for me. I don't want to miss any of these precious moments before her next graduation. That's what life is all about, isn't it? So I'm close to wrapping this post up.

My three graduation words today are Winston Churchill's, "Never give up." (Actually, Churchill said, "Never give in," but it's the same thing to me.) Tenacity keeps me going in the roughest moments we all face.

The greatest motivational speakers all tell us the same thing. Put one foot in front of another. To see what the future can look like in a better, more loving world, and make no excuses. Just get the job done, taking care of others along the way.

I believe there is no such thing as failure, only feedback and mid-course corrections are just fine. Striving for excellence is the only way to go, and being a champion does not come overnight. It takes effort, practice and a can-do attitude.

There is no way I can write anything better than what I just said to you. Impassioned speeches are sure to fire you up and motivate you to excellence. I love speeches that leave us laughing, too, for after-all, when life just seems like things are going downhill, a good laugh changes the momentum for the good.

Selecting just right gifts for graduates? How about the gifts of hope, passion, vision and mission? Most, of all, as you find yourself reaching for the tissues, validate yourself for a job well done, whether you are the graduate, teacher or loved one of a graduate.

It's been quite a year! Enjoy your graduations! Savor every moment! You deserve to congratulate yourself. I wish you all a life of goodness, paying it forward, continued learning and sharing love for those less fortunate, all the things I know you are already doing, because you're you.

Most of all, I hope you continue reading, spread the joy of reading and teach someone else to read or read better. Exactly!

"Congratulations! Today is your day. You're off to Great Places! You're off and away!" Thanks, Dr. Seuss!

Leaving footprints on your reading hearts, Rita

11

PENNIES FROM HEAVEN
February 18, 2017

Do you believe in angels?

Having a strong sense of purpose is important. It keeps us going in the tough times. But surely angels are around to help us turn passion into action.

Rain clouds and rainbows, every cloud offering 'pennies from heaven.' Probably you've heard that classic old song. Lately we've been finding a lot of pennies. It definitely took some looking, as political storm clouds, snows, floods and other things dominated our conversations.

I feel like I'm just catching my breath, so much has been happening so fast. Do you feel like that, too?

Pennies of hope. Belief.

My late husband always told us he would leave pennies around to let us know he was our angel, and that's been happening a lot. I found one in my shoe the other day and my kids report similar experiences. What's weirder is I've been finding random pennies at school, too, some real and some fake from the play cash register. So I'm taking this as a sign, despite some really rough things in the past weeks, the future is bright.

It started with my sister calling with devastating health news, then my daughter's car was rear ended. Out of nowhere I had to put down my beautiful big poodle. I was simply devastated by these life events. Shortly after, our school Director got very ill on a cruise, so I needed to give my all at school, as well as help my family. Multiplicity.

Not enough of me to go around. Life just seems to go like that. Do you ever feel like you are on a treadmill? I had to reframe to a positive place, make peace, find solutions and accept what I cannot change.

Today I am writing from my heart. Great leaders are also followers. We take turns leading and following.

This past week I was, for sure a leader and follower. I was in over my head at school, barely keeping up with the kids, due to circumstances pounding us, that one just cannot prepare for. Sometimes we just need others to prop us up and give us strength. Teamwork.

Teaching is love.

I had the best teaching week. Whenever I'm stressed, I just walk into the school and the world is brighter. Preschool is such a happy place, caring classrooms, with kindness part of the daily curriculum. Because the school has kids aged two to eight, mostly younger, I hope to always be on my 'A' game, especially when we are short our Director's presence, as last week.

I am so happy when I am with young children. Kiddos' innocence and creativity burns brightly. When we talk about Aha! Light bulb popping on, it is obvious with youngest learners, sometimes minute to minute. Any problems, worries or sniffles vanish when I see the kids and start getting those hugs.

The art and craft of teaching goes varoom! I function on auto -pilot until I warm up a little, pieces fall into place. Morning activities, singing, moving, circle time, teaching in chunks, routine and rhythm reassuring, comforting me in my personal loss, doggie tears, daughter and sister worries pushed onto back burners at least while I am with the little learners who demand my full attention.

I found my smile again. Just like always.

Kids are so hilarious. And it definitely brings out my comic side, or maybe I am the only one who thinks that. I'm not sure about that one.

Having a sense of purpose.

I think we all need a sense of wonder. Children boost us up, give us clarity and provide impetus to overcome any obstacle. We are all servant leaders one way or another, giving from heart and soul.

Planning great lessons.

Each day I plan at least three solid lessons, depending on school theme for the day, following the openers. Circle Time is my favorite. I consistently do the following, which seems to be working with the class:

1. Structure and model expected behaviors.
2. Review yesterday's top two things we learned. CFU (checking for understanding).
3. Check or build schema (prior knowledge).
4. Hook to new learning topics for today, to build awareness and make connections.
5. Build interest and excitement with props, music, art, questions, etc.
6. Stories help build fascination, make connections, enhance traditions and ensure memory.

Because the school is multi-age, learning buddies are a significant part of the success of each lesson. All three teachers differentiate, or vary instruction by age and skill levels. There are no set, fixed ability groups, thank goodness.

Lifelong learning, my professional growth.

I discovered that very young children are so smart and can do much more academically than I thought possible. Children who are labeled special needs are also flourishing, which gladdens my heart.

I also learned to get real on expectations. Plan extra, do what I can do every day. Pick the best activities for the particular moment and let the rest go.

1. Expect interruptions. Part of the territory. If a big truck is outside, stop and look. The children love trucks and the outside construction is driving only me nuts. Teachable moment.
2. Hungry children cannot learn. Three meals are critical. Sit with the children, rotate around, encouraging tasting new foods. Model healthy eating with my own lunch.
3. Spills are frequent. Pour minute amounts or milk and water, keep refilling. Teach how to hold cups and use utensils.
4. Hand washing, basic grooming, everything I never thought would matter before curriculum and instruction, matter the most. Kids not having preschool and going straight to Kindergarten are at quite a disadvantage.
5. Literacy predominates. Everything is full immersion about listening, speaking, reading and writing as developmentally appropriate, through play and structured mini-lessons.
6. Recess is a time of discovery, as well as sharing, caring and learning to play fair, by the rules. Outdoor education is a big part of our school's focus on healthy minds and bodies.
7. Children have access to dance, swim, gardening and sports, depending on the weather.

Kindness. Sharing and caring.

I've started incorporating floor mat work with the children, mixing basic 'Brain Gym' exercises with Pilates. Quiet music and calming breathing really worked this week. The school also focuses on positive affirmations. Very calming.

"I didn't do it!" Right.

Thursday was like "Lord of the Flies," honestly. Kids were mean to each other and I saw some bullying that really surprised and angered me. What happened to our polite, following the rules, treating each other gently class?

A couple new girls got added into the mix. Teaming up, nasty to each other. "You can't play with me," and, "I don't want to sit by you."

Not on my watch. Nipped it. Tears. We needed our Director back. She's the glue. I feel like a student teacher with two Master Teachers and Coaches. But holding my own now.

Best lessons.

Teacher Tom and I team-taught several great pieces. I love learning from him.

1. Sharks. Chomp! Oh boy! Kiddos love shark study.
2. Shapes. So much fun making and finding shapes of all kinds.
3. Syllables. We read *Tikki Tikki Tembo.*
4. Word families. (cat, sat, pat, rat, pat, etc.)
5. Math. Counting and writing numbers.
6. Alphabet. Recognizing upper and lower case.
7. States. Kids know states through the letter 'I', and love maps.

Teaching youngest learners is heavenly.

In this time of unknowns in the larger world, I think it is imperative we focus on all the good we accomplish each day, the children we boost up, values we embed through discussion and modeling. This is the most important teaching time of my career, that's for sure.

Thanking you all for the love you share, with the children in your keeping, your school, a sanctuary for heart and soul. I implore you to rest, relax and find balance as you meet upcoming challenges with grace and dignity.

If you happen to find a penny today, 'pick it up and all the day you'll have good luck.' For surely you are heaven-sent.

Leaving footprints on your reading hearts, Rita

CHAPTER 2

LIFE TRANSITIONS: CHANGE INEVITABLE, GROWTH OPTIONAL

Teacher as a Survivor: Life Transitions, Change and Growth.

Chapter Two reveals my thoughts and feelings about moving, overcoming fear, surviving cancer, and spreading grace through legacy. Career stages and life transitions highlight this sweet chapter filled with hopes, dreams and longing, as well as realities of daily life. How Do You Say Good-Bye, Spring Promises, Christmas Love Story, Good-Bye House and Schools Are Gardens for the Heart are some of my favorite titles, because I bared my soul.

- A) How Do You Say Goodbye? Legacy of Love
- B) Spring Promises
- C) Christmas Love Story
- D) Goodbye House: A Story About Moving
- E) Schools Are Gardens of the Heart

2A

HOW DO YOU SAY GOOD-BYE? LEGACY OF LOVE
June 26, 2018

Thinking about my 'Legacy.' What good will I leave behind for others?

"Never doubt a small group of thoughtful, committed citizens can change the world. Indeed, it is the only thing that ever has." Margaret Mead said it so well.

I graduated from preschool.

Well, it's official. I graduated. Preschoolers are now ready for Kindergarten in the fall. Last night I happened to see one of the children with his family at a nearby Mexican restaurant. He looked at me, like "Teacher Rita what are you doing here"?

Maybe it's because teachers are always teaching, parents, grandparents, aunts and uncles, too. We are all teachers, whether in the schoolhouse, at home or out and about. There is always a lesson in there somewhere. And we instinctively know how to teach.

With world events swirling around us, it seems like focusing on health and life's simple pleasures makes sense. Savoring a flower petal, river rapids, hearing wind chimes becomes more important than ever.

And love. Holding dear ones tight in a warm embrace. There is nothing more important. Which brings me back to teaching, our blessing, hanging out with children, looking at the world through innocent eyes, feeling pure, unfettered joy. Problems go away, at least in the moment.

When is it time to stop?

I look at my life and know I not only found my purpose for being, for breathing, I've lived it. Into my forty-seventh year of teaching, one way, one level or another, it's time to stop.

I mean the every day going into classroom, teaching. But that's not easy. That's just what I do. Spending every spare moment, summers, vacations on teaching stuff didn't leave a lot of time for my family. And that is one regret I have and still do. I have apologized profusely to my kids and we are solid, but this is a caveat for everyone else.

Family must come first.

I never retired. My career stages just kept morphing, to and from in the weirdest ways. I was always taking the biggest risks imaginable and most of the time it worked out. Not always. But because my belief system highlights there is no failure only feedback, I just kept moving forward. I still believe that the lessons of the past, living in the now and preparing imagined life skills needed for the future, which is really now, makes sense.

I see people retiring. Everybody has a reason and most certainly should have time to dream, savor life in company of good friends, loved ones and enjoy self-care. Maybe it's just time to take a class, do yoga, dance, sing, garden, volunteer, read or simply take a nap. Or start another career. Anything, everything is possible.

Career stages, yes they exist for everybody.

Career stages have some common trajectories, but sometimes not. In education, business, and other life endeavors, there seems to be a syncopated dance, ebb and flow of newness, excitement, too often boredom, worse, exhaustion, and maybe burn-out. Then we have to make choices.

Teachers on summer vacation are busy in professional development, reading piles of books, attending classes and conferences. Instructors are always planning lessons for the next school year.

Teachers are busy getting donations to equip classrooms with needed resources, supplies and materials. Spending lots and lots of money getting everything needed to teach and reach every child, is a given. I know. I did this, it seems I did so, forever.

Sometimes we say good-bye to a particular grade level, due to shifting populations. Or change schools. Sadly, our position may be cut. Or we don't get hired for that job we aspire to. Or we do get hired and our life alters dramatically. There may be a lot of good-byes, and conversely, a lot of hellos. Usually the only constant is change and the only one who likes change is a wet baby, pretty much.

Once in awhile we meet teachers, business owners and leaders who spend their entire career in one job, one place. But I think, maybe today this is not the case. People seem to be moving around a lot more than I remember, but maybe it's just my imagination.

I always said I would teach until my last breath—and that nearly happened!

I love teaching preschool, which in itself is pretty darn funny. Although I was a preschool Principal a couple years, too, it was never my forte. I decided I could do it, and so I did. I was lucky to be mentored and coached by two extraordinary early childhood gurus. The literacy part I knew how to do, the rest, I learned so much.

And finally I think I was pretty ok, not completely. I was never good with the crafts, never mastered sign language, sang really poorly and trikes running over my feet was not exactly thrilling.

I taught left and right constantly. Getting shoes on correct feet. Putting jackets on, nap mats out. Helping children solve minor squabbles. Treating boo boos with Band Aids. Preschool is the quickest, most challenging teaching I have ever done, but the most rewarding, life saving and soul worthy.

I still am in awe, some of the lessons I taught and at the time wasn't sure were successful. I spent several hours a day planning my mini-lessons, designed to teach basic emergent reading and writing skills, paired with classic books and materials. The simplest things were usually the most effective.

Life was ripped apart. A cancer diagnosis.

Unexpected, devastating illness ripped me away from the youngsters. Pink eye, constant colds were problematic, and so as I fought for my life, although my heart was at school, my body could not be. My plan to finish this year and then decide whether to retire was decided for me, by the higher power.

That still, small voice inside me raged against the night for months. This could not be the end. I could not leave Khloe crying. I wanted to see how much, how well the graduating ten kindergarten-ready children fared, their literacy learning, in particular.

The literacy grant was there. I was not. For months, not just the one or two I expected, but nearly all year, except for a couple visits allowed, I was separated from the kids. And then a miracle. I got well enough to end the year, to finish the year strong, as we say.

To anyone doubting whether teaching, even with pitfalls, fits and starts is for you, find your beginning and middle ground career stage. Rejuvenate this summer, rest, relax, re-imagine and get ready to go back to school with all the joy in your heart. Surround yourself with positive, upbeat colleagues. Have a Mentor and a Coach. Be one.

If you are teaching now, do it for me. Have a grand time making the difference you know you are capable of. Let nothing deter you. Be bold. Take risks. Be fierce. Hold onto that empathy. Your kindness impacts every person you meet in this world. We are better together.

A 'Legacy of Love.'

It's tough to say good-bye, easier to say hello, for sure. I have plenty to do, books I am writing, blogs to read, my family and friends to spend special time with. My health and recovery must be better than this.

As for my legacy, legacy is so intertwined with career stages. Hearing from nearly all teachers I was honored to be with, as Principal, former students, colleagues and friends I met along the way, my legacy is intact as far as I am concerned. I never really thought about it until now.

I look back as I clean out my last remaining teaching closets. I see the stacks of love in form of class quilts, cards, yearbooks, posters, notes, etc. Hearing from parents of high school and college graduates, kids who had such labels they were thought impossible to teach. These kids excelled against all odds. And I am proud. Legacy.

But that takes its toll, eventually. Serving on community boards of directors, the writing, volunteering, teaching, the preparation, only the love lasts when all is said and done. Legacy.

It's not just about finding our purpose, it's about living our purpose with intent and joy. We leave our legacy in every career stage, novice and veteran. By reaching and touching all those we have in our care, schoolhouse, workplace and home, we can do no more.

How do you say good-bye? With hearts filled with love.

Leaving footprints on your reading hearts, Rita

2B

SPRING PROMISES
March 18, 2018

Acts of love

It's been awhile since I wrote for you and I apologize for that. The good news is I'm still here. I seriously doubted I could get out of the mess I was in, no fault of my own. Life happens.

This is not a blog about my illness, and what happened to me, but it does play a major part in my transformation. Only thing is, I'm not done yet. I remain a work in progress. In fact, I will probably send this blog post out in draft. My hands are still kind of shaky, so the very act of writing this is an act of love.

Being on Social Media has been a revelation. After my husband died six years ago, I finished my last book, *Reading Champs,* a how-to skills guide. Then instead of marketing it, I let it sit on Amazon. I started writing again, left my historic home and property in Northern California to move to Eugene. Unreal, for a nester, I moved three times, volunteered, then taught at the preschool. Big changes tumbling one after another.

Family and teaching.

Family and teaching are the constants in my life. Like breathing. My passion. My gift. I've been a 'Servant Leader' for more than forty-six years.

Part of me, most of me would tell you from my heart I lost myself for the past six months. It was a life interrupted due to unexpected illness.

For months I was in my bed, listening to the crackling of the fire and the river outside. My family was taking care of me. My independence was gone. My daughter and son-in law took off work for weeks, staying up with me at night bringing me coconut water and making sure I was ok. Would I make it through the night? I did not know, for such a long time. Never in my worst fears did I dream treating my pea-sized invader would cause such harm; and the burns, unimaginable!

I thought it was enough.

I thought it was enough my teaching was interrupted. I thought it was enough that feeling fine, treatments made me sick. I thought it was enough that I have massive co-pays. I thought it was enough I endured endless tests, procedures and surgeries. I thought it was enough I could barely think and could not write. I thought it was enough I witnessed the sorrows of life in waiting rooms. I thought it was enough I could not focus or read a novel.

And then it happened.

When I thought I was at the finish line. When I thought I was a survivor. When I thought I could bear no more. When I thought I was due for a break. When I thought I made the right decisions. When I thought there were no answers. I gave up. Or close.

Spring promises.

Now I have hope. And when all is said and done, hope is the miracle, the defining moment.

I am sure I was spared because I am not done. I know I have more to give.

I read about the unspeakable things going on in our world, but the goodness I witness every day speaks volumes about the higher natures of people.

Proud to be a survivor, acknowledging things can never be the same, sharing my journey with you is my promise kept. We truly are better together, supporting each other in the commonalities of life.

Three seasons of my journey, fall, winter, and spring. I never dreamed what seemed so simple could be so darn complex, and unending.

Summer bliss, my hoped-for reward for overcoming enormous obstacles yesterday, today, and tomorrow is on the way.

Thanks for making me smile, engaging in collegial conversation, sharing your stories about babies born, alpacas, peanut butter, spam, night owls, and most of all: family.

Leaving footprints on your reading hearts, Rita

2C

CHRISTMAS LOVE STORY
Santa's coming to Town! Naughty or nice?
December 18, 2017

Why me?

I think he goofed on his list this year. I ended up on the naughty column, not sure I'll ever know why. I kept thinking there's a lesson in here somewhere. I haven't found it yet. But small miracles and twinkles, oh yes! Toss in some glitter and wrap paper, a blanket or two and I'm wrapped in kindness and love. I know I can overcome any obstacle, and this is a big one.

It's hard to say and harder to write, but I have cancer. This was a club I didn't want to join. I already lost my husband, brother, best friend, and my sister just finished treatment. Why me? Why now? Sometimes there are just no good answers.

In mid-November, I was leaving school. I just said goodbye to the children about to take their naps. Loaded down with books, craft supplies, umbrella, bags, etc., my cell phone rang. I kept it put away at school, but I was waiting for the news. I assumed my routine test was ok. It was not.

My doctor's call turned my life upside down. Instead of planning lessons for school I lurched into the pink ribbon world, more tests, constant appointments, no time to breathe, going from feeling fine, looking great to being sick. Apparently I was really sick, but didn't know it.

Or maybe even worse. I don't know yet.

It all started out ok, I could handle what I was hearing. I admit I am not a good patient. Leaders probably are the worst. Waiting and waiting. Not liking what I was hearing. A little something kept getting bigger, tentacles reaching out, feeling like "Alien" or "Body Snatchers."

My trike-proof shoes and school jeans were replaced by hospital garb so big I was swimming in it, every test. Surgery is in two days. I haven't been in the hospital except for having my tonsils out and childbirth.

If you ever read (frequently) my commentaries on testing in school, my medical rants would be worse. Now a bunch of doctors, family and friends are cheering me on, convinced I can muster energy to beat this obscene interloper. How can one dot cause so much trouble?

So much for eating clean, a ton of kale, and living in Eugene. Moving to the river this summer I'm thinking now, instead of my sports and Zen mecca, was for healing and to just 'stop.' To come to a forced halt, regroup, do the regimens I have to, and other holistic treatments I have always relied on. My new goal is simply to live awhile longer, hopefully a long while.

I want to live!

My family is arriving. Morgan has a cold but maybe it's better I don't see her right now. I don't want to cry.

Living in the moment.

I have always been mindful and lived in the moment. But now, I am taking it to the limits. I hear every sound so clearly, especially geese flying overhead, the crackle of the fire and the river rapids across the yard.

I barely moved in, was still hunting for socks (not really), but certainly unpacking and organizing when school started. Being a teacher was more important to me than most anything.

I look forward to a lot more special moments here. I feel cheated. I'd been untruthful to deny the stages of anger I went through to arrive at a somewhat more calm attitude. And it's not great, yet, far from it.

Overcoming Fear.

We talk about it, write about it, but when it happens to us, believe me, fear is omnipresent. I was trained and certified in Hypnosis and NLP (Neurolinguistics, the study of peak performance). As a Keynoter I could motivate just about anybody. But this last month I was grumpy, mean, short tempered and not at all like me. I lost me. I forgot who I was. What would my life be like now? When I future paced, seeing my future, it was just negative.

Colleagues, friends, social media were there for me.

I am experiencing unbelievable support from family, friends and colleagues. Social media is especially surprising. This is really amazing to me, that people who connect with us virtually, can also care deeply about one another. The collegial conversation grows into a support system. Celebrating births, marriages, sharing successes at home, school and workplace now seems natural, go figure.

Power of prayer was strong.

I was very negative about my diagnosis, especially as it escalated, and at first refused all conventional treatment. I prayed a lot, meditated as well, and accepted the prayers of others. I believe the Higher Power is sparing me and I hope to better shed grace and dignity on what's happening. I have to accept and surrender that whatever comes next is supposed to be.

So here's the best part, love from my family and friends. Being a widow is not easy on a good day, especially after a long, beautiful marriage. But a widower gets that. And I've been alone a long time now. I think I have a great guy.

None of us truly is in charge of our fate.

I surround myself with white light, saying my affirmations, praying, seeing a fabulous future.

Some days I felt myself sort of in parallel universes. My anxiety was just off the chain. All I can really say tonight is I have had a stellar career, fabulous life and would not do a single thing differently. Our passion, purpose and belief we can make a difference drives us to excellence. With the world swirling around us in unexpected ways, it's easy to throw up our hands and give up.

Each of us sheds light and truth on others.

When we give all we have to give, it is from love. And there is nothing stronger.

'Christmas Love Story,' celebrating life.

I am so pleased to be writing this, my sixty-fifth blog post for BAM Radio Network. As I glance back through the posts, I feel deeply about each one, how I savor mixing things up. Tonight, as I finish this missive, one of my most personal stories, this 'Christmas Love Story' is for all of us, each facing joy, adversity, or something in between.

I thought there would be no happy holiday for me, not true at all. My epiphany is there is a major life lesson. Writing always clarifies things for me.

So here goes, love is all that matters. Love of our students, family, colleagues and friends. Most of all, if we are open and lucky and see what is clearly in our face, maybe someone special has been waiting.

Wishing you all an abundance of festivities, warm embraces, and the gift of love. See you soon!

Leaving footprints on your reading hearts, Rita

2D

Goodbye House: A Story about Moving
July 10, 2017

So go figure. I find everything else but the missing socks!

Where do those socks go, anyway? Now that I finally tossed the odd ones, will the mates turn up?

Gotta' keep moving.

I've never been so organized as since I moved into this tiny (to me) house, used to bigger spaces and maybe grander places. But for two years I rented this vacation house, not by the beach but in glorious green South Eugene, to be honest, really for my big poodle, Gus.

Right near old growth trails and ferns, dog parks, lots of places to explore. Deer and turkeys are abundant. This area reminded me of my old California property. I thought this might be home. Check it out awhile, give it a test, then maybe buy it.

Even has an old chicken coop on the side, but I was asked not to use it. Made no sense to me, since barking dogs all around are far noisier than chickens. Little house on terraced property. Inside 70's architecture, interesting features, woody. I really fit in here and mixed it up, a combo of Eugenian hip, with old Chinese antiques.

Morgan's sleepovers, plentiful, which of late are no big deal now. She's a pro. Everything organized, dolls, blankies, and surprises. Six years old and now a firstie.

I love the book *Good-bye House,* 1986, by Frank Asch. Funny thing is I've been placing it around, all over the house to maybe generate a little interest. During night reading I showed Morgan the cute cover. No way. She doesn't want to read it yet.

Hopefully we can read it next sleepover, before I take our sweet, crazy, cozy little house apart to move somewhere really special. Or maybe not read it. I'll have her pack up all her stuff, like we've been talking about. However, we need one more time together, everything in its place here, the way she likes it.

To be honest, I have to make it easier for me, after this hard winter of freezing rain and losing my big red poodle. I do best with a wood stove or fireplaces. I'm not into coming home ever again to a thirty-two-degree house with a non-functional pellet stove. I already had no power for a week!

I moved closer to my kids and school, by a river. I won't need to play Soundscapes. Just open a door and a lot of other valid reasons. I just did not want to make anther move right now, but here I am, doing it. I'm figuring it out day to day.

This winter was a rough one, the last months more turbulent, with choppy waters to navigate. Time to let go of this house. Make the effort for something new. Starting over is looking pretty 'rainbow' to me. A permanent vacation, there are so many amenities and a kitchen big enough my take-out days are limited.

Still, it's hard for Morgan, at six with those two front teeth out and knowing every nook and cranny at my house. Properly placed stools, towels out, her little office space set up. She made centers of sorts, little maker spaces, her Barbie dolls are around, of course, also her library and art area. She stashes stuff I find later in weird places. Everything will be different soon.

Sometimes I wonder if she remembers Papa and our California mountain cabin home. I know she loves the pictures and hearing our stories. Life continues. Generations.

With a nod to Albert Einstein: "Life is like riding a bicycle. To keep your balance, you must keep moving." That simple statement is so profound.

Everybody moves. Some more than others, like me.

Sometimes we just have to. My house is freezing all winter, about 6 months a year. Reason enough.

We move for change, renewal and growth. There are lots of kinds of moves.

Sometimes we change schools, grade or content to stay fresh and challenged.

And lots more. Moving is change. Change is inevitable: growth, optional.

How I'm doing.

Ok. I'm still in the middle of the tunnel, but seeing some light. I'm behind on visiting my friends and family, reading blogs and paying bills. I'm cleaning out every drawer. The hose connector broke and water is spraying all over except on berries, at the moment.

Our family has serious life stuff going on right now, so I'm feeling like Gumby, pulled in a couple directions. I've shed a lot of tears lately, then I pop onto social media and looking at silly posts and motivational photos is like instant pep talks.

Teaching at preschool, year two.

I stayed! I have until mid-September to get myself caught up. This year I know I can do a better job. I learned so much about teaching youngest children. I really miss the daily joy jolt of love. Our master teachers continue to mentor me.

Are you moving right now? Ask your students, too.

Big changes. If you are at a high transient rate school, there are always lots of kids moving, and maybe homeless, too. Bunches of children are moving back and forth between parents and grandparents, aunts and uncles.

Moving transitions. Transitions are part of life.

It's far easier to advise how to do necessary interim steps than to do it myself. I'm making the list, checking it twice, or thrice, hoping Santa is good to me this year.

Self-care should be number one.

Take naps or breaks, whatever you like to do. I did today, after a massage, long overdue, and a chiropractic adjustment, then a two hour nap. Yesterday I spent an hour at the community acupuncture clinic.

I was crumbling, starting to feel overwhelmed. Rightly so. But this is not the night I want to talk about it. I'm feeling so positive and future ready.

Future pace. See it, hear it, feel it. My new life.

For me, I see myself no longer sticking my hand into a hole to turn on a valve to water the side yard. Weeds, moss, and what went with all this rain. No more lugging bags of pellets. I do my Pilates stretching and a lot of tapping and breathing.

Mindfully, I see myself recreating and repurposing, with more room, two fireplaces, and best of all, the river. I hear the rapids, like putting a seashell by my ear.

Morgan went a couple times to see where I was moving. She picked out her room (Not happening). Of course she wanted to be in the bedroom by the river, the fireplace room. Mine.

Her room will have favorite dolls, puppets, most of my antique school collection, the little brass bed. I see it already. I am seeing how to make it so cozy. I can place Papa's old desk in there. Morgan already started hiding her art supplies. She likes it!

This will be her new office, with all its interestingly shaped special big and little drawers and opened up, it has a work area. I unlocked it. Smart move. I thought I really needed that desk, filled with memories, but better it goes to Morgan. We just have to figure out the highest piano bench or chair to reach everything. But she's crafty. A pillow or two may be needed.

Moving adventure.

I'm making a lot of to-do lists. Keeping just what's necessary, if the other half of the coffee pot didn't show up by now, it's not going to. I keep filling bags and boxes to donate to a couple local charities.

I need to buy shelf paper, a lot of lining to do, not sticky stuff I can never measure right and get it stuck together. I also must notify post office, insurance. Oh no, just writing this stuff I'm going to give myself a panic attack.

Breathe. Stay calm. I can do this.

Everything will be just fine.

Goodbye House

When all the furniture was packed in the moving van, Baby Bear said, "Wait a minute. I think I forgot something," and he ran inside.

"Come on" said Papa Bear, "let's say goodbye," and he picked up his son and carried him from room to room. They said goodbye to the dining room...and the stairs. They said goodbye to the ceilings and the walls. They locked the front door and said goodbye to the whole house. And as they drove away, Baby Bear said, "That's what I forgot. I forgot to say goodbye."

Frank Asch. 1986

Wherever you are moving, or taking a road trip or vacation, just keep moving. Make sure to rest and have play time, too!

Happy summer to you all!

Leaving footprints on your reading hearts, Rita

2E

SCHOOLS ARE GARDENS FOR THE HEART
April 17 2016

National Poetry Month and the gift of hope.

Spring is a time for rebirth and new beginnings. As we pull the weeds of winter, we reflect on our learning successes, assess, plan and hope for the next year. Gardens are a grand way to teach children sequence of life including planting, tending, and watching that garden grow: just like learning.

Tending the garden of the heart.

Teaching is cyclic and routines offer us continuity. We share our rituals and routines with the children in our care, offering much needed stability and a gentle kind of love and nurturing wherever it's needed. And that's pretty much everywhere, one child at a time, for various reasons.

I love class or morning meetings, circles or whatever name you use. The time is well spent. Even five minutes sets the tone for the day, with a quick review of prior learning (especially helpful to an absentee) and transition to the next activity. This is time worth spending. More than time on task, definitely engaged. Engaged in emotional safety and sense of class belonging and visibility. Tending the garden of the heart.

Lately I've seen some really cool school gardens. When I was Principal, a garden was already at the school, a good beginning. We added a wildlife compound and accomplished many project based learning activities, at the time not putting a name to it.

Like our favorite book, *The Carrot Seed*, plant some seeds. I guarantee when you properly tend those seeds, they do come up. Eventually. Time is a big factor. Some students just take more time to learn things. Many times I experienced a teacher doing every imaginable strategy and no numeric results. Then voila! That proverbial light bulb flashes in neon, maybe even the next year or so.

I still believe in the work of Rita and Kenneth Dunn, Marie Carbo and Thomas Armstrong. It seems so obvious that multiple ways of knowing are important. The notion of learning styles and multiple intelligences always made sense to me; there are some question marks about their validity, today. I think children all show their gifts in one way or another, when given the opportunity. Certainly there are many ways to be smart, and schoolhouse learning is just part of life.

Today's curricular garden is vast, with a lot of expertise out there. I like the idea of blended learning, a mix of technology, with carrots and peas planted, probably some string beans, too. Inquiry anything, as I've said previously, adds kale and spinach. What do kiddos want and need to know and how to achieve that? That's the only real curriculum in that schoolhouse learning garden.

Being in nature, doing the math and spatial concepts needed to get those poles strung just right, figuring out how much and when to water, fertilize with TLC. Learning to be patient. Can't beat that natural kind of learning. Cross- curricular, internet search and hands-on, minds-on projects are in alignment with scientific method.

And, providing opportunity for students and teachers to pose questions to each other, higher level thinking questions. Lessons are designed to ask questions and solve problems from a most literal perspective to one of more introspection.

Moreover, the tactile-kinesthetic spatial elements being satisfied, and basic needs taught to us by Maslow, gardens provide the maximum teaching opportunity. Adding in writing, poetry, art, and music about the gardening experience, is perfect learning extension. Let our spirits soar!

How to assess the lessons?

Honestly, anecdotal. Seeing happy kids, free to explore, in their genius hour, in developmentally appropriate ways, how joyous! That's assessment.

Then the harvest.

Learning in the school garden is a festival of celebration. When children taste the garden vegetables they tended, there's the 'Aha!' moment of moments. See the ultimate flow state in action.

I also love to see flower gardens at schools. Adding beauty that blooms off and on, is awesome. Another bonus, gardening offers a lot of practice in sequencing.

Children of all ages and stages are the ultimate blooms. One of my favorite classic books is *Leo the Late Bloomer*. I so identify. Maybe we all do. All kids learn best, differently. Leo takes time to catch on, then he blooms, like the flowers, plants, and vegetables in the garden.

My 'rule of thumb' is to teach everything at least three times in three different ways. Also, offer children opportunity to design and assess their own learning, and decide what they want to know next. And so on. Gardens offer lots of learning opportunities.

'Life Lessons' in the garden.

I don't believe in failure, only feedback. I rarely make it through a single day without making some sort of error or having a new obstacle thrown in my path. I think that's true of everybody, don't you?

Sometimes gardens don't work as planned that season, so there's a lesson to be learned and changes made. Nobody has to buy in, it's all obvious. That's what happens in good schools with shared leadership.

Taking walks with children, working in gardens, painting maps and dinosaurs on the playgrounds are all garden tending. The planning and execution of these school projects offers a variety of reading, writing, math, thematic curriculum at its best. Gardens of the heart.

National Poetry Month,.

Reading a daily poem to the class about gardening, including student written, is fun. I'd do a language experience lesson for the littles, writing down what they say about being outside, then reading it back to them.

Sometimes time-tested strategies are so classroom perfected, keep the learning traditions that help kids flourish. That's garden tending. Old and new seeds mix. Traditions matter.

Moreover, gardening adds a *Yo, Yes?* friends! school and class culture experience. Kids work together with buddies or teams, may cross match with other classes. Schools sharing their gardens classroom to classroom via technology is the ultimate.

You might have fun doing *Flat Stanley* gardening projects, integrating every imaginable learning aspect. Pens Pals can be more than just electronic.

Fine and large motor opportunities involved in tending that garden help reading. There's actually some perceptual and tracking opportunity. It's also a kind of phonemic awareness lesson, with its rhythmic rhyme, rhythm and repetition elements. Haiku!

School culture is enhanced with gardens. Watching schools bloom means students bloom. Happy teachers, staff and all stakeholders feel the love, determine academic success and make it happen.

The process of shared 'visioneering,' closely followed by a renewed Mission Statement plants those beginning seedling packets. Start with a nucleus of seed pods and the growth will move from there. It's like watching corn grow.

I'd start with something like this:

- To build a school that is safe, calm, and without hunger.
- To build a school where learning is the primary goal and failure is not an option.
- To build a school where routines, rituals, celebrations are the norm of the school climate.
- To build a school where all voices are heard, especially those quiet ones, who have important thoughts, too.
- To build a school that is a sanctuary for the child, in every way.

I have so many memories of hanging out with my Dad, gardening.

When I was a little girl I planted pansies with my father. Some of my happy memories of that house and time on Clinton Street revolve around digging in the dirt, hanging with Dad.

I'll bet all you gardeners out there are planting those seeds right now for spring revival and rejuvenation after class tending all year. A lot of flowers and vegies are blooming right now.

I'd like to extend this lesson with the idea of a School Farmers Market, with parent and community involvement. Consider the many opportunities.

Schools are gardens of the heart. Thank you, gardeners.

As I picked my azaleas this morning, I was so thrilled they finally bloomed, all in brilliant color, just radiant.

Leaving footprints on your reading hearts, Rita

CHAPTER 3

LEADERSHIP AND SOCIAL CONSCIENCE
Teacher as a Leader: Leadership and Social Consciousness

Chapter three is about strength, standing up for beliefs and sharing a collective voice for what we need to accomplish in our community, country, and world. I am a risk-taker by nature and speak out for justice and equity. As an educational activist, there were many stories I wanted to write, and some I simply couldn't bear to write. I did manage to put pen to paper, so to speak, on a number of major social issues that I found deeply disturbing or significant, like school shootings, DACA, Charlottesville, bullies and Title IX, the school-to-prison pipeline, equity through inclusion, and more.

A) Should Teachers Get Purple Hearts?
B) DACA Dreamers!
C) Charlottesville: How Did We Get Here?
D) Everybody's Gotta' Go! But Where? Transgender
E) Hands Off! Title IX
F) NEA's Stand: Just Say No, School-to-Prison Pipeline
G) Hometown Inclusion Hero

3A

SHOULD TEACHERS GET PURPLE HEARTS?
May 26, 2018

Memorial weekend. Safe schools for kiddos. Heroes in waiting.

But could you do it? Could you face a shooter and pull the trigger? Or tackle someone? And not panic? Tough questions. It's fairly easy to say what we would do, but could we do it? Our split second decision lasts forever, with so many ramifications.

School shootings are unfortunately the new reality.

As of now, eighteen states allow teachers to carry firearms, undoubtedly there will be more. Obvious concerns including insurance companies worrying about liability, teachers questioning the idea, incidents already occurring with teachers making errors with guns, pretty inevitable, and the social dilemma of what to do next about this growing and heinous problem.

In 2017, there were forty-four school shootings we are aware of, elementary and high school. The grisly toll was twenty-five lost and sixty injured. Thus far this year, statistics are horrid, twenty-eight school shootings, with forty deaths and sixty-six injured.

Just another day. Another shooting at school. Yesterday's shooting was at a Middle School in Indiana, a bunch of innocent kids. The shooting occurred in a class taking a science test in their classroom. Not just any classroom, it happened to be Jason Seaman's, a former football player, school football coach, and most importantly, science teacher. Mr. Seaman was hired to be a science teacher, not a hero. But hero he is, however unintentionally.

On an ordinary school day, a kid in a teacher's classroom asked to be excused for whatever reason and came back with two guns. Guns he used, which severely injured one young girl and shots ended up hitting this brave teacher in his stomach, hip and arm. Jason Seaman most likely prevented more injuries by thinking fast. What we hope we would all do. But he went beyond being a servant leader. He offered up his own life to save his students.

It seems like Jason Seaman, extraordinary teacher and human being ought to get a Purple Heart, except he is a teacher, not in the military. Valor beyond the call of duty. This cannot be the new normal for our nation's teachers.

I read a number of stories about what actually happened in the classroom on Friday, and most accounts to date are the same. This teacher and class had practiced for the event, should it ever occur, but I imagine they thought the danger was from the outside, not in their own class. One of the students said the shooter was basically a nice kid and got along with classmates. So what in the world led to carnage?

School and safety drills.

While schools across our country are practicing safety drills, in the larger world arena, politicians, parents and school leaders are pondering what to do. So many issues are involved, not just about changing gun laws. Let's add in discussion about mental health and stress of our students, worried parents and exhausted, flummoxed administrators and teachers.

Apparently Jason had told his class earlier in the year he would 'throw down' and hit any intruder with balls, or whatever it took to subdue, and that's what he did. Exactly.

What a hero, throwing a basketball, wrestling one or more guns and tackling the student. I can't imagine. And I am reluctant to contemplate how students felt, the panic, seeing their teacher save lives by his unimaginable valor. There are no words for this. No words at all.

And what did this bravest of brave, teacher say when he was conscious, about his kids? "To all the students, you are wonderful and I thank you for your support. You are the reason I teach." Such humility. The mark of a true teacher leader.

Have we come to this, after the headlines, business as usual. Numbed, accustomed to chaos, it seems like it's getting a lot more risky to just be at school, teach at school or send our kids to school. Scary.

It used to be we were just worried about snow days, then making sure we had peanut free zones. We worried about test scores. Worried about too old school buildings and class sizes too big. Feeding hungry kids, working so hard to level the playing field. Transforming schools.

Model mindfulness, acknowledge resilience.

Teach real life, useful skills. Help kiddos be future ready for the brave new world workplace, whatever that may look like. But not about protecting ourselves from gun violence in our safe havens, schools as sanctuaries of the heart. Safe zones of learning for our scholars. School cultures designed for celebration, not intimidation and fear.

Yet here we are, thinking where is the closest exit? Where can we be safe from an intruder? Anywhere?

Even with plans in place, the inevitable has happened. Old classrooms have more than one door; frequently there is simply no way to block an intruder. Classes are proverbial sitting ducks. From without and within. What's a teacher to do? Heroes and sheroes all, as needed?

Other duties as required?

It's so unreal. To hear about another school shooting. Then another and another. We kind of get numbed after awhile. So many lives lost. So much untold promise not met. Sorrow and grief for always and ever. While there are some commonalities, we're not sure who or what is to blame, or where to start, to solve this problem.

School districts may be adding gun safety training for all or some teachers, or none. School Resource Officers are certainly needed. Lower class sizes help teachers to more readily spot a kid having a mental issue. Put nurses and counselors back in schools. Reach out to local universities to coordinate Counseling and Social Work Interns for districts and schools.

For years I taught School Administration, for California State University, Sacramento, National University and Chapman. The first tenet I stressed in our courses, before curriculum, was straight from the California Education Code, "Safe and orderly environment" and "Duty to Protect". And that as Principals, we were responsible for children's welfare from the time they left home until back at home after school.

Oh boy, it's tougher now, that's for sure. And it was tough way back then. When I became Principal there were bullet holes in the school and it was a very rough neighborhood, but I never feared for our safety and certainly had no gun, in fact no cell phone. I was gutsy. I made a lot of home visits by myself.

I am sure administrators are wringing hands, making sure every possible safety measure is in place and hoping the tide turns. It must. Even the best prepared schools have still had extreme events. What works now? Metal detectors. Or? No answers yet, these are pretty much still local decisions.

Firearms Safety Class? Yes, I took one—for preschool!

A couple weeks ago I took a Defensive Firearms Class, not for concealed carry, but I needed certification for school. Yes, preschool! Anybody who works or volunteers now needs to take the class. I passed the test, missed two. I was not expecting to have a test, but it wouldn't have mattered. This, all new to me was not much about common sense, at least for me.

Class was held in a classroom, not on the range itself, and we were not expected to shoot. The Instructor, a former Marine was excellent. I learned about basic firearms and how to keep them clean and in working order, with proper bullets. I learned a lot, as I had no real 'schema,' or prior knowledge. I had practiced shooting a gun before, for safety at our mountain home, but I am not personally into guns. I would not trust myself, even after the course. No way. Trust that.

I was the only one in class not wanting to carry a gun for protection. I knew nothing, had no schema, no prior knowledge. So my head was spinning. I asked the Instructor whether he thought teachers should be armed. He replied, "Hell no." This was sketchier than my CPR class. I felt really secure there and saved my doll. But this was different.

One of our Instructor's comments really stood out: "As a private citizen you have no duty to act. Nothing says you are required to get involved because you have a firearm on you." And yet, that is exactly what we are expecting teachers to do, with or without gun safety or self defense training.

It takes a lot of practice to shoot well. We were told it takes about a thousand repetitions just to get used to the kinesthetics of shooting. As I said, I can shoot a gun, I have always chosen not to.

How many teachers already have a gun and might want to be considered for a school response team? How fast could these elite people prevent or stop an intruder? Is that a new part of a teacher's job description, 'Other duties, as required?' That used to mean volunteering to host a school club. There is a big difference.

After this tragic event, several extremely valid points were made on Friday night. The most obvious, this story had not focused all day on the bravery and heroism of this one special teacher. In fact, during the day I never caught a news story, nor saw it on Twitter trends, nothing. By Friday night I was aware there had been another school shooting. Maybe I missed it. That was it.

A colleague asked, "Even with training, faced with an active shooter, what would a teacher actually be able to do?" Teachers are supposed to teach. It seems enough to work in underfunded schools with overwhelming odds, yet teachers do so admirably and are every day heroes and sheroes, to begin with. And now this.

I heard from another teacher on Twitter. He commented, "Rita, hi! Combat veteran here, seven deployments, including four tours in Iraq. I teach now. I shouldn't be shot at, and simply, I shouldn't have to charge at ANY shooter anymore. There shouldn't be shooters for me to charge heroically. Would I? Yes, but goddamn, no shooters, please!"

"I'm not sure I understand what you are trying to say. I have never taken a bullet, never been shot at, and as much as I'd like to think I'd be as brave as this teacher, I can't answer that, and I hope I never have to do so."

What about Purple Hearts?

Should teachers receive Purple Hearts? Probably yes, but no. Purple Hearts are, of course, reserved for combat-wounded soldiers, and rightly so. But is this where we are? Is this what our world has come to? Teachers accepting responsibility above and beyond the call, sacrificing themselves and family because of passionately protecting students from any and all harm?

I have no answers, only more questions today, on this Memorial Weekend. I thank this amazing Teacher Hero; his cape was definitely on.

Our nation's teachers are already wearing capes, capes which are wearing out, becoming threadbare as educators finish the year strong with passion, love and teaching excellence. We cannot ask our teachers to do any more with less, and certainly, not this. Take a bullet? NO!

It's just too much to contemplate and more than we should have to bear. We are beyond thoughts and prayers. We must figure this out. Our very lives may depend on it.

Leaving footprints on your reading hearts, Rita

3B

DACA Dreamers!

September 4, 2017

Labor Day: Si, se puede. Yes we can!

DACA refers to 'Deferred Action for Childhood Arrivals.' Until recently, perhaps we were not as aware of this program as we should, or could have, been.

Earlier in my career I taught school administration in the Bilingual Cohort at California State University, Sacramento. I was Keynote Speaker and trainer many times for Migrant Education, Mini Corps. I worked in bilingual classrooms under Title Seven Grants in Sacramento and on the border, in San Ysidro, Ca. I was also privileged to be lead teacher several summers for residence Bilingual Institutes, at California State University.

I was mentored by Dr. Armando Ayala, big dreamer of dreams. He was my colleague who encouraged me to learn Spanish and understand culture and challenges, including some of the family situations now coming to the forefront in the DACA issue. I missed attending the Language Institute in Cuernavaca and admit my Spanish remains minimal. However, I firmly believe in cabeza y corazon, 'head and heart.' All my teaching situations were intended to motivate and help students of all ages and stages achieve their lofty dreams.

I guess I can just say my heart has always been in a special place with the enthusiastic young people I met, and taught with. There were always tears and so much love. I have no idea whether their parents were legal, illegal, citizens or not.

I had one contract in a border school I particularly relished. I stayed with the school Principal. Everyone spoke Spanish in her house. Total immersion. Every day their friend walked across the border from Mexico to stay with them, then walked back across the border at night. This was more common than I knew. Yes, a very big issue.

America, the beautiful. Land of immigrants.

America has always been a place of dreams, big and little, sometimes meshing together, sometimes not. Once in awhile we get what we want right away, sometimes our hopes and aspirations are deferred.

America is our country of dreams and dream makers, builders, movers and shakers. We all have opportunity to exercise our freedoms and leadership and this is one time I am requesting we come together, as a nation, on behalf of three quarters of a million young people, who know only America as home.

Thinking about children and young adults who know nothing other than this country. Who may be your child's math teacher, or a fireman saving lives in Houston floods.

I understand the complexity of this subject and once again, this is perhaps held hostage in a political arena of bullies, back to Dr. Seuss' book, *The Butter Battle*. A time of walling in and out, isn't that enough already? Reviewing paths to citizenship may call for a reform of some sort, but why ruin lives of 800,000 young people many or most serving their country, this county in some helpful, meaningful capacity.

The numbers are truly staggering. It's not simply eight hundred thousand we're talking about here. There are mamas, papas, tios, tias, hermanos, hermanas and so many family members potentially affected by this morass. Grandpas and grandmas, documented, undocumented, mixed families, some legal, some illegal, some who thought they were safe under DACA and now live under a shroud of fear.

Do we really want to show our lack of diversity, civil rights, compassion and true review of all ramifications and issues involved here, before a life altering decision is pronounced by our nation's decision makers?

Or deferred, causing months or hopefully not years of humiliation, fraught with worry of deportation or mixed family deportation. And how would we, could we as a just nation deport the Dreamers who followed their program to the letter, who had near perfect records, not criminals or miscreants.

Children born in this country or brought as a baby or a little one, who know only America as home, being deported to an uncertain future in Venezuela or somewhere else. Interesting, Canada has already offered asylum to these young people.

I believe in legal immigration of course. I recognize the sacrifices and rocky paths so many have ventured through. My purpose tonight is simply to add thoughtfulness and compassion to something so important to us: our respect as a nation of learners, leaders showing our fiber and moral compass. Isn't a wall enough? When will it end?

On this Labor Day I send an urgent request for diligence and laser-like focus on this important issue, dignity and respect for all residing on our shores.

DACA Dreamers. Thank you for your belief in the goodness of the American people to hear your pleas, share your stories and offer sanctuary until wiser people than me figure out what to do. In the meantime, everyone please slow down, gather your strength to weather the storm and find a most happy ending.

Leaving footprints on your reading hearts, Rita

3C

CHARLOTTESVILLE: HOW DID WE GET HERE?

August 12, 2017

God bless America, Land of differences.

Bigotry, hate, violence, is it possible to find common ground for real dialogue when the country feels like it has gone mad at the moment?

Violence did indeed break out at today's White Nationalist Protest. Not surprising after the disgusting images I saw on Twitter last evening, late into the night, ahead of news media. It was inevitable. I followed Twitter threads until 2 a.m., in disbelief.

As of this missive, nineteen injured, one deceased. A state of emergency, currently called by the Governor Of Virginia and city officials, bringing in National Guard. Am I imagining this? In the year 2017???

Chants, including, "Blood and Soil. Jews will not replace us. You will not replace us." Repugnant! We cannot allow this. Snaking lines of tiki torches, vile signs, violence. Displaced anger. I wish Dr. King was here to lead us out of the darkness and into the light.

This started over removal of a Confederate statue, or so we thought, free speech at odds with common sense emotions, not leading to unmitigated violence. Does the right to protest immediately guarantee horrendous clashes among protestors and counter protestors, protected by law? What happened to the greater good of race relations espoused and modeled by Dr. King, Gandhi, and many other great leaders?

There comes a time when we must all take a stand for what's right and true. That time is now. I see no point in reviewing all that happened last night or today. By now, you have caught up one way or another.

And the history we witnessed is not pretty. And it's not fake news. People injured and killed, Americans raging at other in the night and in the day. No hoods, faces openly staring back at us, Americans, brothers and sisters, no more.

Years from now, of all the despicable rhetoric spewed recently, whether on social media, or elsewhere, in real time, will we ask, "how in the world did they let it happen?" Sounds familiar, just like what happened in Germany, maybe?

Our heads are spinning from the constant bombardment of negativity in a time we preach love, mindfulness, being a Joyful leader in our schoolrooms. We write and model positive mindsets, no bullying and getting along with one another as a major needed skill for success in future, ever changing careers.

We teach grit, resilience, never giving up. We also teach that there is no failure, only feedback and we make mid-course corrections at any time, as needed.

Well that time is now, and I don't mean just about schools. Look at any Twitter page and the majority are filled with positivity, happy children learning in varied classrooms, with great fervor, not wanting school days to end. That school is a party, the best celebration in town. And hungry children are fed, clothed and cared for by each school community, with cultures supporting building program capacity.

Never fully funded, schools do an amazing job preparing their kids with the sense of belonging, caring for each other, understanding differences make us special.

Our nation is a nation of immigrants. My family originally came from Latvia, Russia and Germany. And yes, I had family who died at Auschwitz. So let's just say I, too have experienced the victimization of mind blowing, ignorant, coarse hatred because of my religion at various times in my life. "Funny, you don't look Jewish."

Although my mother warned me against marrying a Christian man of German descent, we had a blissful marriage, never dwelling on our differences, only similarities.

When I was in high school I went to a school where most of the Jewish kids went. For high school prom we could not attend one of the big hotels because Jews were not allowed. In college I could not get into any sorority other than the Jewish one.

My husband William, as I said, was raised Christian but we never had any issues raising our four children. My point is, hating anyone who is Jewish by birth, or by differences of any sort, we miss what being 'an American' is.

We are a melting pot. You should sit at our extended family table. Everyone came from somewhere else originally. We look different, talk differently, have different beliefs, but hate can't be a trait we espouse as a nation.

What in the world is going on? Where did all this hate come from? Was I on another planet? What are the implications for educators, on the nation's frontlines with children every day? What kind of curriculum do we teach at every grade level to counter the extreme hate currently evidenced, truly out of our control and purview.

How do we discuss and explain the series of events on a college campus sacred ground, the importance of a long past symbol, the Civil War maybe happening again, to an extent. Oh, my.

One day we hear about Russia dismissing our ambassadors, with Russia, Korea, and Venezuela swirling in the background. The wall, rounding up immigrants, transgender military ban, etc... not just hovering, but actively dismantling our American way of life every single day, one way or another.

We see afterschool and nutrition programs being cut, and attack on our public school system, teachers leaving the profession due to lack of respect, constant useless testing and simple burn out. Amazing administrators and teachers do remarkable work under constant Reptilian threat. Unacceptable! I laud our profession.

As a nation, we're decoyed by intense subject matter, guaranteed to garner our interest, watching our nation's holy grails chipped away; maybe book burning next. Children of poverty are expected to excel because of their resilience; teachers are creating miracles each day.

Teachers and communities step in, support and fund the unfunded. Class sizes matter. Teachers need adequate supplies and capability to teach without interference. And don't start me on changes in the Department of Education, not so positive, in my opinion.

I flipped news on recently one night and saw a story about our Ambassadors in Cuba slammed by mystery audio waves affecting their brains. Are we in an Orwellian alternate universe right now? Have we turned into the movie "Idiocracy" by no fault of our own?

How did it happen? You tell me. I just watched and listened. I wrote about Henry's Story In my blog, "Hometown Inclusion Hero," I talked about "Title IX," wrote about bullies and suspensions in "Butter Battle". It was not enough. I commit to step up to the plate.

I even shared my concern about our Supreme Court and transgender kids' toilets. But I am clueless tonight how to fix this mess and need your help.

It's great to write and focus on the positive, but it's time to stand up and shout out. "No More."

I never dreamed I would be writing such a personal blog post tonight. How do I dare not? How do I sleep later, a restful sleep with visions of torches lined up on a college campus, holders yelling, "Blood and Soil!" Please look this up in Wikipedia. Nazi references are clearly there. How terrifying.

America. Now. Not the 1930's again. "And then they came for me."

I implore leaders to stand up and speak out against what happened the past two days. It must not happen again. It cannot.

Thank you, BAM Radio Network, for providing this platform to brainstorm our best response as a united group of educators, stakeholders in our nations' well being, and returning civility to the collegial conversation, ending anger and violence we witness.

Spewing hate and discord is certainly not what we have been modeling and teaching in our schools.

There are no disabilities, only capabilities. What religion does it matter as long as we believe in something other than a world of hate? Love is where the action is. Loving one another, cherishing, our differences, which bind us as one people.

Emma Lazarus gave us the gift of love when she penned: "Give Me Your Tired, Your Poor, Your Huddled Masses Yearning To be Free." I thought we all believed that. I guess not.

Last night I had been watching 'The Great British Baking show', laughing at the fact I don't bake. I decided to go up and read for a while and opened my laptop. There it was, report after report of unexpected violence on a college campus, not sure whether this was about the Confederacy, KKK, fake news, or what the heck, could this possibly be America in 2017???

No media outlets had picked up this blazing story of guys carrying tiki torches, (how tacky), chanting "Blood and Soil," cursing Jews, immigrants, people of color, anyone different than white.

Did 'Make America Great Again' really mean Make America White again? For goodness sakes, what about Rosa Parks, Dr. King, all our heroes and sheroes who sacrificed so much for our country.

Our differences make us unique, stabilize us, offer a plethora of beautiful opportunities to learn, share and grow as one people. We are not divided. We are one.

I am not taking sides or making political statements tonight. I simply want to share my sorrow at the turn of events in our country, coming not slowly, but rapidly.

I would prefer to be writing a sweet, frothy back to school post, which is what I had intended. Instead I find myself sleep deprived, deeply confused, shocked to the core witnessing the heinous acts as unmitigated anger manifested in violence.

How can we, as people of good conscience not stand up and speak out? I would like to see each and every teacher and administrator this week, discuss Charlottesville. As a collective force we have power to turn this around. Schools filled with love counter hate. More than ever, we are all leaders, including parents and our local communities.

We must immediately contact our representatives who seem to be clueless or spineless at the moment, not all, of course. Thank you to the courageous politicians who represent our interests, political party not mattering, adherence to basic common decency and humanity is what counts.

A time for unity necessitates every single person, every American to denounce this untoward, cowardly, demeaning, threatening behavior whether on a college campus, in a school or the larger community.

Churches, mosques, synagogues are a great place to start, book clubs, online study groups, our counselors, superintendents, school boards, in short, everybody in our collaborative communities must be involved with fervor and genuine commitment. This cowardly behavior is not going to extinction by ignoring it. No way.

Hope. It is always about hope. It cannot happen again. Not here. Not now. It is time for a united, collective vision not just of excellence, but man's humanity to man, or whatever gender designation we choose in our free country.

As educators we must all speak out, loudly and clearly with sure and steady voices. We must ensure safe and orderly school environments, cultures of love, forgiveness, empathy and belief in a better world for all. God Bless America.

Leaving footprints on your reading hearts, Rita

3D

EVERYBODY'S GOTTA' GO! BUT WHERE? TRANSGENDER
About transgender teen Gavin Grimm and the simplest civil rights issue of all: Which bathroom to use?
March 10, 2017

I never thought I'd be writing about bathrooms.

It was not exactly my favorite part of being a Principal. But it still mattered. A lot can happen in a couple minutes in an unsupervised bathroom. Bullying is usually out of sight and I doubt there are cameras.

I admit I have gone in men's rooms on more than one occasion, when the women's lines were their usual snake down the corridor. But I have never had to worry on a routinized basis which door to enter.

When I have Morgan, our Kinder with me, she knows to walk into the door with the picture of the skirt, not the pants door. But what if she decides later that she really wants to be with the pants door?

After raising four kids, I understand how a parent feels, being mama and papa bear to protect our unique children. Really we are all the same, and we owe respect to any and all variations in society at large, at home, and in this situation, at school.

First and foremost, all schools are obligated to provide a safe and orderly environment. All staff have a 'duty to protect.' Providing safe schools is number one priority. Before culture. Before curriculum. Before all else.

When I wrote my Title IX blog, I had no idea all the ramifications and facets it truly covered. I believe it protects the civil rights of LGBTQ students, but I'm sure that is subject to interpretation. We're about to find out.

I do know that school administrators and teachers need direction how to best support the rights of transgender students. On February 22, 2017, the Trump administration took back President Obama's decision that transgender kids should use the bathroom (or locker room) matching their identity, not necessarily birth gender identification.

The face on the debate.

This greatly affected one teen, in particular, Gavin Grimm, beginning nearly two years ago. Gavin, who came out as transgender in 2014, simply wanted to use the boys' bathroom, matching his gender identity. He was a sophomore, and didn't want to change schools, as suggested.

The rural Virginia school, after hearing from enough parents, told Gavin he could use either his own designated bathroom stall, or in the nurse's office. Gavin decided to sue. For about two years the case has been working its way through the courts and finally made it to the Supreme Court.

Gavin did not intend to be the face of a national bathroom debate. He simply wanted to be heard.

This week, on Monday, the long awaited answer did not arrive for Gavin. Nor did it arrive for parents, the LGBTQ community or schools. We do not know whether Title IX does, in fact, protect these vulnerable students, depending on interpretation. It certainly should, as it clearly prohibits discrimination whether by touch or words, no bullying. Hands-off.

Title IX.

Title IX provides major Civil Rights protection for all children. It bars sex discrimination in public schools but does that extend all the way to transgender students?

The Supreme Court decided to send the case back to the U.S. Court of Appeals for the Fourth Circuit due to new circumstances. It is such an important question reaching into bathrooms, showers, locker rooms, etc.

Apparently until the February 22, 2017, Presidential order, Obama's 2016 position on transgender student rights formed the basis of prior decisions favoring Grimm and his cause. What will happen now, or next is vague and unclear—except that the Appeals Court will have to review and reconsider the case.

Until then it appears inconsistent local policies will guide how transgender students are treated. It adds a burden to School Boards, Principals who may be making decisions on a case by case business and opens a Pandora's box of vulnerabilities regarding possible lawsuits.

The reality, to me is that all our children deserve respect and have a right to identify with gender, not necessarily birth identification, as boy or girl. We cannot meet educational needs until Maslow's basic needs are met.

Transgender kids are bullied.

Attempted suicide rates for transgender community is thought to be 40%, 50% for those who were bullied at school. Children of color may be at even greater risk.

The guideline reversal may have slipped past us with all recent events shaking our Country. Changes are coming fast and furiously, whether we agree or disagree.

It is not my intent to make a political statement of any sort, simply to help create a larger awareness of this argument. Additionally, I hope we stand up for these children with or without support of Title IX, just meeting our moral and ethical obligations as parents, educators and members of the larger society.

When we talk about growth mindset and a positive school culture, reaching and meeting the needs of all students is top priority. Let's keep close watch on the kiddos in our care who need to use the bathroom, just like we do. It's part of the human condition.

Transgender children know whether they identify as male or female and that decision has to be respected and protected.

There are many sources of information for you to read about this important issue.

Yesterday, advocacy groups and several parents of transgender students met with Education Secretary Betsy DeVos. They shared concerns about the removal of gender protection and told stories of the torment and depression suffered by their children.

I certainly hope bathroom usage is not a political issue, but a children's civil rights discussion. I'd love to hear your thoughts on the subject.

I also hope to learn that the Education Secretary who already expressed some concern before signing on to the elimination of former President Obama's guidelines, mitigates the situation in some meaningful way.

We make the difference in the learning lives of all children. I believe we are all servant leaders, hopefully making sound decisions and forming solid judgments based on truth, merit and, simply advocacy.

Leaving footprints on your reading hearts, Rita

3E

HANDS OFF! TITLE IX

October 22, 2016

"Keep your hands to yourself." The first rule we teach our preschoolers is a good start. Manners and appropriate behavior have to start somewhere.

I read a shocking article about Title IX I couldn't wait to share, not another—minute. This is a shorter post than usual, but I have a lot to say.

As a principal, and when I taught school administration, the first tenet was to ensure a safe and orderly environment. 'Duty to Protect' was clearly stated in the California Education Code and I took it seriously.

Before we attempted any process of developing a Vision and writing Mission Statements, lofty goals were put on hold until we secured our school from outside, inappropriate people and events; and inside, how to get along together as family.

It's important discuss the importance of anti-bullying and creating intact, thoughtful mindsets for appropriate behavior.

Gentlemen Clubs, counseling, class meetings and many programs have been put in place to stop bullying and protect the wide diversity of students in our care. Digital citizenship is an appropriate topic. What times we live in.

As a member of AAUW (American Association University Women) I was already aware of the 2011 study and findings about unwanted sexual harassment in schools and on college campuses. It is not my purpose today to take this topic over the top, but draw your own conclusions.

I tutored one little non-reader who is now a student at Cal Poly. He was scarred by an incident in Kindergarten when he was cornered by an older boy in a bathroom. Recently, Morgan was scratched repeatedly on the kindergarten playground...the last incident leaving welts on her back, through her jacket. Bullying starts early, innocence lost.

The national election brought out troubling commentary I am obviously not dealing with here, but perhaps it is a catalyst for national conversation. Once again, the onus returns to us, as educators, parents and members of the collective community.

Jane Meredith Williams, shared a thought provoking article in *EdSource*, July 24, 2016. She relates the AAUW study painted a grim picture of what we must deal with. The statistics are shocking, nearly half, forty-eight percent, of grades 7-12 in the sample of two thousand students, reportedly experienced some sort of harassment based on gender.

Girls were more likely than boys to have negative experiences, but not always.

This is literally against the law in federally funded schools under Title IX, the Title IX Amendment of 1972, reiterated in 2011 from the U.S. Department of Education, Office for Civil Rights.

Title IX is not just about sports, but also applies to sexual harassment, assaults, etc. In other words, protecting our students from unwanted advances of all types, including touching, words, and more.

Brett Solokow, Executive Director for Association of Title IX Administrators, suggested that about 85% of schools may be out of compliance regarding providing a safe and orderly environment for student learning.

In 2013, the California Department of Education sent a letter to all school districts requiring Title IX Coordinators to complete a survey, but response was so low nothing was published.

Schools are obligated to act.

It seems obvious that this is a complex issue, to be properly weighed by all school personnel, with positive plans reviewed and perhaps new directions needed due to a changing world landscape, or at least one that has now flown dramatically in our faces, in the best interests of all children.

I was not aware Title IX had these facets, but it gives us a starting place. It's the law. Moreover, despite our best efforts, perhaps we can do more, starting today. Every school continually works in shared leadership moving forward in so many curricular innovations. This has to move to the top of the list.

Kids need to feel safe.

When all is said and done, kids of all ages, pre-12 need to feel safe walking down halls, on playgrounds, using bathrooms, in classrooms and online. We are already champions for children, now even more is required.

I see this as a civil rights issue for more than grades 7-12, it's the right of all children. How we get there is up to us, but changing the landscape is perhaps even bigger than test scores and the myriad of other tasks we embark on. We spend so much time, and rightly so, developing amazing curricular programs, teaching positive mindsets and self-regulation, children managing their own behavior.

We face the bigger societal issue of how we treat each other as humans, regardless of how we look, our religious belief, the language we speak. We are ONE!

Leaving footprints on your reading hearts, Rita

3F

NEA'S STAND: JUST SAY NO;
SCHOOL-TO-PRISON PIPELINE

July 8, 2016

I met Leslie Van Houghten.

It's not something I often talk about. Tonight, it has resonance. There comes a time we must reach deeply into our hearts and souls and reflect on common truths.

Recent violent events in our country trouble us all. I know we wake up and wonder what's happening next to test our patience, unsettle us as a nation, try our core values as a collective people.

We wonder how to help our children living in poverty, how to level the playing field and bring us together as a village of leaders and learners. Our Vision and Mission for safe, well fed, educated children is more important than ever before.

Before I was a Principal and Curriculum Consultant, for a number of years I worked in penal education. It just happened. Starting as High School English teacher, it was apparent too many kids couldn't read well, or at all. One thing led to another and there I was teaching Reading and getting my Masters in Reading. My thesis was on delinquency and the non-reading correlation. Paths go in circuitous routes sometimes.

I worked for Arizona Department of Corrections, youth and adult, Title I program for inmates under 21, then California Department of Corrections, the real deal. I 'walked the line' at Deuel Vocational

Institution, taught with cell study teachers at San Quentin, visited all prisons at that time with younger inmates. Our hope was to catch young people with aspirations for a better life and provide intensive academics, in particular how to read.

My first visit to a prison I met Leslie Van Houghten. I was told she would never be paroled, but that's questionable now. She was working in the school office at the Women's Institution. I vaguely saw the X on her forehead, but never dreamed she was one of the infamous Manson girls. As a Program Evaluator, I traveled to all the prison programs, including in remote camp areas, I had to take tiniest of planes to get into the desolation.

I don't know now how I did it. Young family, scary places, just a strong will to maybe make a difference to those I served. Once you get into a prison it feels so weird and unsafe, regardless how many times one does it. More importantly, kudos to forward thinking institutions which believe in rehabilitation, not just punishment, or I would not have had opportunities to test my faith.

I met some interesting inmates during those years. Most of all, the dedicated teachers working with scarce materials, hostile work environment and institutionalized mentality, deserve medals.

I like to think the Elementary Secondary Education Act of 1965 (ESEA Title I) made a difference. I doubt many of you realized that Title I was originally intended and extended beyond public schools into the most unimaginable places. I was there.

My life's work has always been to work with the neediest of the needy; in particular, the kids no one wanted, because I get it. They were hard to deal with, disrupted their classrooms, and unglued teachers. I just like that kid the most…sometimes.

A number of studies cite stunning differences in discipline referrals, rigid restitutions and out of school suspension for children of color, most quoting at least three times more. What should be a huge concern to us all, corporal punishment is still allowed in nineteen states.

Bringing tears to our shared eyes, many children are in effect beaten, in about nine states, primarily. One is too many. Don't you think? The actual numbers are staggering. There are so many studies to pick from. I was shocked when I started the research, and I thought I was already pretty expert on the subject.

Looks like the school-to-prison pipeline is no joke.

It's real, with tentacles into many societal ramifications, both negative and positive.

Recently I wrote a blog post about kindergarten suspensions. This is a worthy read, highlighting the increasing number of kindergarten suspensions, and suspensions, in general. That starts the ball rolling, just the proverbial tip of the iceberg.

I loathe writing with such venom about children being beaten, in this day and age, when my last two posts were so feel-good about letting go of our floaties in life, preschool, and graduation.

Be sure to take a look at studies regarding racial inequality and school discipline. There are so many of them. (You can start with Wikipedia.) I am simply aghast as I write this, but I do want to give you some food for thought before you take action.

What can we do? There are alternatives. Let's share the good things that are happening. It's time for a serious dialogue, for the kids' sake. Whenever possible, we need to keep the 'challenging' children in school, whatever it takes. Thank you NEA, for taking a strong stand and offering ways to reach true equality.

Leaving footprints on your reading hearts, Rita

3G

HOMETOWN INCLUSION HERO
High School Graduation
May 29, 2016

Once in a while we meet a 'Henry.'

He may be your child. Henry inspires and teaches that we all belong together. Tonight I am writing about Inclusion, in particular, one young spirit who overcame many obstacles, and his devoted mother. Mama love. Get your tissues, this story is like *Rudy, Rocky,* and every feel-good inspirational book and movie, ever.

Before I moved to Eugene to be with my kids, my husband and I had a historic home in the middle of nowhere, Northern California. There were a couple of towns nearby, but our house was a kind of hangout, with a pond, barn, community gardens, wildlife, and berries. I was teaching at nearby Chapman University, and tutoring a lot of kids at the property. One day Patricia Storrs brought Henry over to work in the garden and see the house. He had been reluctant, fearful of the 1858 ghosts, including Mark Twain.

Henry stayed in the car for over an hour. Patti and I checked on him, let him garner courage, and then he walked the property, house and had a great time touring on his own. It was joyous seeing him emerge from that car and do his thing. I knew that day that Henry is special, in the very best way.

Henry is a hometown hero.

While Principal, we had the District Learning Handicapped class on our campus. First thing I did was move the kids from the trailer in the North Forty right into the middle of our campus. Our students were fully included, or nearly, most of the day and participated in every school project, club and activity. The class was in charge of the wildlife compound outside their door. These kids were our Henry, believe me.

I am not an Inclusion expert. But tonight, Henry's story is our story. His graduation was our success. In a moment, I'm sharing what his mom wrote for you. I am very grateful to Patti, his principals, teachers and most importantly, all the kids along the way who did not bully, but accepted Henry's unique differences, discovered his wisdom and became fast friends. Henry is a Hometown Hero, for sure and a champion in the best ways imaginable. We have a lot to learn from him. Tenacity. Love.

Henry graduates High School, by Mrs. Patricia Storrs.

Yesterday I had the joy of watching my son Henry graduate from High School. A much more emotional graduation for me than usual, as it was an event I wasn't sure would ever come to pass.

Henry was diagnosed with Autism Spectrum Disorder at age 4, and although he was a verbal and absolutely delightful child, we had some initial struggle in getting him settled into his neighborhood school. He was a little high maintenance: he would stand at the window of his kindergarten classroom waiting for me to return. Or stare out the window from his desk, distracted by every bird or airplane... When it was suggested that he would be better off in a special program, we fought for him to be included at his local school.

The special program was far from home and populated mostly with kids who were older and much more severely affected by ASD. In Henry's particular case, we strongly believed his needs would be best served by being immersed in his community. More than reading, writing, and arithmetic which comprises the main educational goals of our 'typically developing' kids, Henry most importantly needed to learn how to fit into his society. How to make friends. How to live his life as a 'square peg in a round world.'

So we worked hard and the school responded. My mom's strong convictions kept me going when I weakened (it's hard to be the only non-professional sitting at a long conference table filled with people who are disagreeing with you!). Long story, but we prevailed. Henry won. He spent academic periods in the onsite special education program, but had a homeroom where he started his day, and joined his class for lunch, P.E., recess, library, music, story time and field trips.

Henry moved on to the local junior high without a blip, surrounded by kids who had known him since preschool. When he moved to the much larger high school, those same kids set the example for everyone else, and defended him when needed. But not much defending was needed. Henry's delightful personality wins over everyone he meets. He became a beloved member of the student body. And he did learn to read, write, and do math to his capability. He has loved school throughout. He loves his friends (and he has so many!).

Most importantly, Henry is happy. Henry was basketball manager for two years. They called him 'The Commander' and named a new perpetual award after him, 'The Commander Award' for inspirational manager. Then he was recruited as a football manager, too, senior year. He won 'Manager of the Year' for all sports this year!

As a postscript...at Henry's final IEP meeting at the local elementary school, the principal cried. He apologized for not seeing back in kindergarten that the school was the right fit for Henry. He said, "I can't thank you enough for what Henry has brought to our school, and taught all of us, students, teachers, everyone, about inclusion and acceptance. He has been so good for all of us."

Henry's proud mom, Mrs. Patricia Storrs

Full Inclusion for all. Make it a reality.

Beth Foraker, Supervisor, lecturer in the Credential and Master's Program at UC Davis, California is mother of a special child. Beth, who is also champion for full inclusion in Catholic schools and all children, wrote me something very significant.

"These ripples of inclusion cannot be overstated. For typical students to see what's possible with access and support for people with disabilities creates a mind shift that can't help but influence the rest of their lives with an inclusive mindset.

That is everything. Work for inclusion every day—we are all better when it happens. Just look at the possibilities!"

To all graduating students, families and loved ones, congratulations! Joyous, happy tears.

Leaving footprints on your reading hearts, Rita

CHAPTER 4

READING: THE GREAT DEBATE CONTINUES

Teacher as a Researcher: Celebrate My Passion: Reading.

Chapter four is not only informative, but also offers compelling rationale why we need to promote reading without tests, These collected stories suggest reasons to end the great, unending debate on how to teach reading and offers practical strategies for anyone teaching or coaching reading. You can practice speed-reading hacks, enjoy summer reading ideas for family fun, and find out how to appreciate the classics at home. I have included a couple interesting articles about boosting reading fluency, not retaining third grade challenged-readers, and the problem with too-early kindergarten reading instruction.

A) Speed Reading Hacks!
B) Way Cool Summeriffic Reading
C) Family Classic Reading Time with Junior Novels!
D) Fluency
E) Should Struggling Third Grade Readers Be Retained?
F) Dick and Jane Go to Kindergarten. Yikes!

4A

SPEED READING HACKS!

November 5, 2017

For the first time, maybe ever, I can't keep up with my reading.

My stack of novels grows, but I don't speed read these. I savor every word. Reading for information is different, I can adjust my rate to match the material, and routinely do so. I find myself reading a mixture of info-text online, newspapers and books. I don't use a Kindle. Just never wanted to. I always liked the feel of a book in my hands, pictures, the miracle of what lies in between the covers.

I also spend time popping onto teacher and leadership chats, reading blogs, checking my emails, reading links to various research sites, both good and not so good. My two Facebook pages are time intensive. Besides cat videos, I scour a lot of relevant research on various things I'm interested in.

We spend time working with kiddos on their reading rate and fluency. I'm thinking now that we all could stand a refresher course, how to pick up our own pace, to meet vast needs, keeping current in our minute to minute changing world.

The future is now. What works for kids, works for us too, so use these reminders for your students or yourself. You might enjoy online or old fashioned personal charting of your increased speeds, by following one or more of these success secrets.

Basics: What do you already know about speedier reading?

What do you already know? What do you want to know? After you confirm your learning, you'll want to know more. This is just a snapshot glance at closely connected subjects of fluency, rate and speed reading. There are so many definitions of fluency, starting with 'automaticity,' automatically knowing a word.

As we advance in literacy, there is so much more to know about which words have most meaning, signposts and signals, etc. Let's just get started.

A 'good reader' is flexible, matching reading skills, purpose and rate to read fluently. Intonation, phrasing and emotion, are also important. However, improvement in the physical, mechanical aspects of reading makes a huge difference. This includes rate, rhythm, shortening time of each eye 'stop,' and increasing the width of vision-span-per-eye-stop.

Mechanical aspects of reading.

Way back in 1879, A French researcher, Javal noticed a student's eyes don't move smoothly along a line of print; instead they make a number of starts and stops every line. These are called 'saccadic movements.' Although these eye stops only last one-fourth to one-half of a second, the pauses are real and easily noticed. Meaning is made during these stops, the pauses that inform. Too many eye-stops, however, and speed and comprehension are affected.

Everyone can improve reading speed skills, once the fundamental building blocks are mastered. You can watch your students while they read, or catch this for yourself. You watch, or someone else watches. Observing the number of stops along a line helps us move our eyes faster, taking in more information at each eye-stop, phrase, a complete sentence, or later a paragraph.

A certified Hypnotherapist and NLP (neurolinguistics, peak performance) practitioner, at one time I studied 'Photo Reading.' Ostensibly, by altering our 'state,' through a kind of self-hypnosis, we could conceivably 'photograph' an entire page at one time. I was never able to do this, although I was reading remarkably faster.

Speed readers greatly exceed 900 words a minute by skipping words, lines, and whole blocks of print. We really don't need to read that fast, do we? Reading in which all words are read can't be done much faster than 800-900 words a minute.

This is supported by the fact that the shortest possible fixation when reading two-to-three words, is at least a quarter, to a fifth of a second, in duration. This would mean that a ten-word line would be read in two thirds of a second! For our purposes, picking up our pace, or rate, by reading in phrases, whole lines, and paragraphs is enough, don't you agree?

Hack that reading speed.

1. Observe your student's (or your) reading along a line of print, online, or textual, noticing the number of eye stops, or fixations. Your goal is to lengthen the span and lessen the number of stops. Dividing the number of fixations by words read is the 'index of recognition span,' or amount seen per fixation.

2. Eliminate back skipping, or 'regressions.' It slows down reading rate and lessens comprehension. Use a metronome to pace, or tap a pencil to set a rate or rhythm. Recording reading is very helpful. Partner reading also works well. Forward and backward motion reduces speed as much as 30-50 percent.

3. If your student labors with reading, has trouble tracking print, makes continuous errors, reads one word or one syllable at a time, mechanics becomes a top priority. Do Echo Reading, (Reading under one's breath, along with student) Repeated readings, (150-180 words), three times, in two-minute increments. Graphing is successful to show progress. I think the reason why it works is the process of 'overlearning' kicks in big time.

4. Use easier, familiar reading material, books, and technology. Why teach at the frustration level?

5. Go back to phonemic awareness and phonics, if needed, to fill gaps. End reading letter by letter, word by word reading. Watch speed zoom!

6. Sub-vocalizing, saying each word out loud slows down reading. Actually, whether orally or silently. Encourage using eyes only, without moving head, or mouth.

7. 'Retellings' not only encourage comprehension, but boost fluency. The more familiar with material, the faster the reading. Use small chunks of two or three paragraphs to a whole page.

8. Hold the book or tablet up at a 45-degree angle, instead of down on desk. This helps eyes take in more print at a time, and there are frequently less eye stops and regressions.

9. Give skimming and scanning special attention. When skimming to survey material in the preview, notice headings, first and last sentences, etc. Great time for a full Book Walk for preview.

10. Let your eyes run down the middle of the page to gain an overview, stopping once or twice on the line. This is called 'Super Dipping.'

11. Focus on the white spaces between the lines, rather than the lines themselves. This is called subliminal reading, or 'reading for concept' (reading between the lines). Brain-based.

12. Or, focus right above the line of print. 'Tangerine Effect' refers to softening your gaze. You will be amazed how fast and how much you recall.

13. Practice 'Tri-Focus' Read it Fast.' Set up a practice sheet with three columns, asterisks across and down page. The student 'reads the stars,' then applies strategy to reading material with the student reading larger span based on a tri focus of three columns, as practiced.

14. Scanning for specific information. Use the 'Crisscross Method.' Scan from top right corner to bottom left corner, then glance at top left and scan to bottom right of page.
15. Provide a written selection, telling student to insert vertical lines between words to highlight proper phrasing.

Perception as basis of speedier reading.

Perceptual means the number of letters your eyes can perceive and understand in a single sweep. The greater the span of perception, the more you can read in a single glance. Most readers have a perception span of about 20 letters, about four words. We can do better, necessary in our high speed, high tech world.

Final hacks.

Practice rapid page turning, when applicable. Skip the little words. Stay away from the margins. Rate is determined by purpose. So know why we are reading something. That helps us adjust our rate.

No doubt about it. If we are going to keep up in life today, we have to enhance our own reading speed skills. The very volume of media, documents, contracts, life stuff print alone is staggering, at least to me. I bet you, too! Hope these hacks help you.

Leaving footprints on your reading hearts, Rita

4B

WAY COOL SUMMERIFFIC READING
May 22, 2016

One of our favorite books at the moment.

Pete the Cat and the Magic Sunglasses, by Kimberly and James Dean, is one of our favorite books at the moment. Anything Pete does, rocks! This 'cool cat' looks good in his sunglasses, offering us life lessons as he shakes off his blue cat blues and learns to see life in a whole new way. That's what great literature does for us: it helps us see people, places, and events in colorful, insightful ways.

Summer offers time to be with our kids, reading, writing, enjoying library visits including maker-spaces and 3D printers, reading for the fun of it, with first books, chapter books, young adult literature, classics, non-fiction, and graphic novels. Road trips are perfect for audiobooks. Books go on picnics, camping, shared reading under a tree or in a hammock, anywhere and everywhere.

iPads, Kindles, Nooks. Just read.

Set the stage for reading success at home.

1. Turn your home into a print and language-rich environment. Create book nooks, crannies, forts made of boxes or blankets. Read in a little tent. Offer an invitation to stop and read. Books introduce us to other people, places, and cultures. Our

imaginations run wild with excitement as we meet characters like us or so different we can't wait to see what they will do next. This is the beauty of fiction. Encourage reading non-fiction, too.

2. Create smart little readers by reading! Start reading to your baby right away. When your kiddo is a toddler, lap reading is not only heartwarming but an effective reading strategy. Your little is watching your eyes follow lines of print, notices you reading from left-to-right, hears your expression, and is immersed in the joy of reading. For pre- or emerging readers, read books featuring rhyme, rhythm, and predictable patterns. As you read, point out that sounds make letters and letters make words. Sing along and use puppets or rhythm instruments. Unleash your creativity!

3. Continue reading with your children long past toddler stage. When kids start reading on their own, it's still important to read together. You build vocabulary, boost comprehension, fluency, and model can do attitude and joy of reading.

4. Check the book's reading level. Books need to be at an independent reading level. The easiest way is ask your child to put a finger down on the page each time there's an unknown word. After five fingers are down, switch to an easier book. Children reading at a frustration level don't understand what they read or won't want to read.

5. Start family classic reading time. For fiction reading, let kids self-select favorite books. I like *Captain Underpants*. However, I am also a true believer in classic literature.

6. Sharing great literature will be remembered as a family tradition. By turning off electronics a set time each day, you set the stage for lifelong reading success. Make a family reading goal: books you want to read together and post a reading record of what you read. While you are reading, stop and discuss the book. Do One Minute Book Reports. "I like this book

because..." Discuss characters, plot, setting, and theme. "What did we learn from this book? Do we like the book? Would we recommend it to others?"

7. Read a variety of non-fiction. First, know your child's background knowledge. Next, take a Book or Article Walk, noticing author, date, new vocabulary etc. As you read, make predictions or guesses, then read to find out if you're right. Finally, summarize. Stop after each chapter, page or paragraph. This boosts comprehension. Reread if necessary, doing repeated readings.

8. Immerse your developing readers in a weekly theme or topic. Read fiction and non-fiction; use library books and Internet articles. At the end of each, share what you learned. Themes reinforce family values: love, friendship, loyalty, courage, heroes and heroines, discovery, invention and adventure. Have your kids provide examples from their reading which support the theme.

Hacks for figuring out your child's reading level.

Independent reading level: With fluent reading, word recognition errors (miscues) don't exceed more than one per 100 words of text, with 90% or better comprehension.

Instructional level: Assistance is needed. Word recognition errors don't exceed more than five per 100 words of text. Comprehension would be 75%.

Frustration level: Student understands less than 70% of the reading and you may notice physical or emotional discomfort.

If you want to read a book or article with unknown reading level, make an educated guess.

Check out the length of sentences and complexity of vocabulary. Generally, an easy selection contains short sentences and simple words, a more challenging title has longer sentences and abstract words. Illustrations contribute greatly. Look for colorful art.

Type size counts, too. It's measured in points. Select easy on the eyes type styles. Leading (sounds like 'leding') is the space between lines. Larger spaces are easier to read. Lines that are too long cause more eye fixations and slower reading. You can use readability formulas, of course, but this is more cumbersome and maybe not too accurate.

Sometimes a book is too hard for your child, but if there is a burning desire to read that selection, just do it. Provide lots of support though.

Hacks for learning new, unknown words, any age or level.

Read the whole sentence to see if there are some clues to what the word might be. See if any part of it looks like a word you already know. Cross check, Does it look right? Sound right? Make sense? Are there any known words in the word?

How does the word begin and end? Is it a compound word? Is there a prefix or suffix at the beginning or end of the word? How many syllables are there? Are there any word families (little word in the words, like at, in cat or hat)? Sound out the letters using cues, or hints. Use context clues (words we know around unknown word). Ask for help, last. Look up the word. What's its definition and origin?

Sampler of favorite classic books for the littlest reader.

Madeline, Five Little Monkeys, Stone Soup, Rosie's Walk, Everybody Cooks Rice, Tikki Tikki Tembo, Last Stop on Market Street, Strega Nona, Stellaluna, Are You My Mother? Ira Sleeps Over, Jesse Bear, What Will You Wear? Brown Bear, Love You Forever, Millions of Cats, Corduroy, Bear Shadow, The Carrot Seed, If You Give A Mouse a Cookie, Caps For Sale, Make Way For Ducklings, Chicka Chicka ABC, The Very Hungry Caterpillar, Yo! Yes? Rain, Leo the Late Bloomer, The Little Engine That Could, Goodnight Moon, Go Dog Go, The Snowy Day, Froggy Gets Dressed, Dr. Seuss books.

Classic chapter books and junior, young adult (YA) novels.

Amelia Bedelia, James and The Giant Peach, Charlotte's Web, Sarah Plain and Tall, Stone Fox, Matilda, Hatchet and The River, Sign Of The Beaver, Call of the Wild, Patty Reed's Doll, Harriet The Spy, Dear Mr. Henshaw, Caddie Woodlawn, Number The Stars, The Lion, The Witch and The Wardrobe, Island of the Blue Dolphins, Tuck Everlasting, Bridge to Terabithia.

Summeriffic reading offers a perfect combo of reading for fun, learning new information and polishing skills. Have fun responding with technology, drawing, writing, sketch- noting, singing and dancing. Check out local book clubs, special reading programs and events. Most important, snuggle up and read!

There's no summer slide, only a glide for our young readers. Rock on, you family reading rock stars! Happy summer!

Leaving footprints on your reading hearts, Rita

4C

Family Classic Reading Time with Junior Novels!

December 8, 2015

Classics are classic!

I believe in focusing on time-tested, values laden, keen adventure adolescent literature. Classics are classic!

Literacy instruction is now leaning more heavily into info-text. I highly question the movement away from literature. Certainly a blend of pleasure reading and textual material seems a perfect match, like peas and carrots.

Once kids start reading on their own, you can't beat *Captain Underpants*, joke books, non-fiction, such as volcanoes and sharks or graphic novels. But today I'm talking about classic core literature, time-tested beloved junior novels, which always delight and make you think.

By second or third grade you can start moving into family friendly novels from early reader or short chapter books.

Parents, it's important to keep reading long past toddler time. The 20 minutes a day pleasure reading goal is a good baseline. But why not add in another 20 minutes to read a chapter a day of a novel, as a family? You can even sneak in a skills mini-lesson.

Scholastic Publishers shared informative research about the importance of continuing reading to children past toddler years. As I recall, five-to-seven days a week, 91% of parents read aloud to their toddlers. Not surprising. Yet only 54% read aloud to three-to-five year old children. This declines to 34%, for six to eight year olds, and only 17%, for nine-to-eleven year olds. What do you think about this? And what can we do about it?

Why not read a family novel a month?

I suggest you read and share a family novel a month. Yes, it's possible. Even with crazy busy schedules, read after dinner or during 'stolen moments'. While anthologies and excerpts are ok, it's far better to read entire books. Take turns reading out loud, summarize what's happening, share feelings and connect with other favorite books.

My favorite Junior novels, time-tested and still relevant.

1. *Matilda*: (Roald Dahl) (varies, mostly grades 3-5)
2. *Stone Fox*: (Gardiner) (2-4 grades)
3. *Charlotte's Web*: (E.B, White) (2 plus)
4. *James and the Giant Peach*: (Roald Dahl) (3-8)
5. *Tuck Everlasting*: (Natalie Babbitt) (grades 5-8)
6. *Dear Mr. Henshaw: (Beverly Cleary) (grades 5-6)*
7. *Sarah, Plain and Tall: (Patricia MacLachlan) (grades 2-4)*
8. *Island of the Blue Dolphins*: (Scott O'Dell) (Varies 4-8)
9. *Bridge to Terabithia*: (Katherine Patterson) (4-6 grade or older)
10. *Harriet the Spy*: (Louise Fitzhugh) (grades 4-6 or older)
11. *Hatchet* (and *The River*): (Paulsen) (varies, 4-9)
12. *Number the Stars*: (Lois Lowry) (varies, 5-8)

The most important goal is to read great literature as a family tradition. A secondary benefit, you model the building blocks of basic novel reading strategies.

Basic teaching hacks for novels.

- Plot: "This book is about....It begins with...The middle part is about...Here's what happens at the end."
- Story Grammar: Who? Where? When? What? Anchor it. Who are the main characters? Where does the story take place? When does the story take place? What is the problem? How do the characters resolve the problem?
- Sequence: Storyboard map: Fold a piece of paper into 6 boxes. First. Next. Next. Then. Then finally! (Or make a sequence chart: record first, next, then, and finally.) EASY. Hold up a finger for each of the steps or stages.
- Setting: Before reading: Where do you think the story takes place? During reading: Has the setting changed, or is it the same? Before and during: When does the story take place (day, season, month or year)? After reading: Describe the various settings, if there were any changes in the book. Thank about it: How does the setting add to the story? Would this story be different in a different setting? Draw the setting.
- Character: Make a basic web, or circle with seven spokes. In the middle circle, write the character. Spokes include: How old; Looks like; Family; Friends with; Says Things Like; Acts Like; Problems are?
- Make Predictions: Use this frame out loud, or written: Guess what it's about. "I think that it's about..." Read it. "I was right. I wasn't right. I was sort of right." Make another guess. "I think that..." Read it again. Continue this process until you've finished the chapter or book.
- Figurative Language: Start with basic comparisons: (metaphors) and similes (like, as).
- Summarize: Combine with retellings, summarize often, keeping the flow of the story. Make 8 box folds out of paper. Or fold into sixteen boxes. Use as many boxes as needed to

summarize each paragraph, page or chunk. Write one short summary in each box.

- <u>Vocabulary</u>: Pick out the best new vocabulary in each chapter. Make lists, or index cards defining the word. Practice spelling and using the new word.

Classroom teachers encourage pleasure reading at home. I'm suggesting for only twenty minutes a day, turn screens off and read some classic adolescent literature. Family classic reading time will be a fondly remembered tradition! I promise.

Leaving footprints on your reading hearts, Rita

4D

Helping Kids Build Fluency and Joy of Reading!
November 15, 2015

Reading out loud builds fluency.

Just say no to flat, expressionless, boring reading. Say yes to smooth, correctly phrased, lilting lyrical reading! Here are some easy-peasy ideas for you!

Where and when do you start?

Read to your tummy. No kidding! Next comes lap reading; keep reading with your child long after that. This is the first step toward building fluency. By modeling your love of reading, children hear the lilt in your voice, see your expression and experience the joy of language.

I always encourage family reading time, as well as bedtime reading; reading together is the perfect way to enhance fluency.

Following along with online stories is also helpful to see the pictures and hear the words at the same time. Many classic children's stories on the Internet are really enjoyable. Using audio books during car trips can be inspiring for your kiddos. Nothing beats hearing great readers sharing stories.

What exactly is 'fluency' and how do we encourage it?

Its very definition keeps changing. For example, researchers at one time thought fluency meant a child had no word identification problems. That meant the children had no problems recognizing new words. Others stated fluency meant bridging word recognition and comprehension.

Since the definition of fluency continually evolves, form your own opinion. What do you think it means?

In a mechanical aspect, fluency means '*automaticity*,' immediately knowing the words and getting meaning from print. First, a budding reader is 'automatic,' then becomes 'fluent.' Developing readers enhance their fluency through lots of practice and repeated readings, reading the same paragraph or page several times to pick up the pace.

Fluency also means reading orally with appropriate speed, accuracy and feeling. We encourage kids to read in phrases, smoothly, with a lot of expression.

A little more to think about:

- Silent reading must be fluent, as well!
- Fluency changes with familiarity of text. New text slows kids down.
- Fluency affects comprehension. More fluent readers know what they read.
- Reading word-by-word and '*regressing*' (back skipping) loses meaning.

Fluency testing in school is very stressful for many children.

Find out how your school assesses young readers. Often children read to a teacher or teaching assistant. Your child must read a certain number of words correctly, with expression and smoothly, not word for word. I get that. But it's challenging for a new reader and often the child doesn't want to read after that. So it's important to minimize stress, schoolhouse or home. If your child is incorrectly placed in a non-rotating reading group, that's not good.

Here are ideas for your teaching toolkit for youngest readers.

1. Read together, out loud.
2. Let your child self-select the book, at least part of the time.
3. Teach classic picture books and early books.
4. Focus on books featuring rhyme, rhythm, and predictable patterns.
5. Practice reading in phrases. Model it with your child.
6. Use a metronome, or tap out phrases (beats) with a pencil.
7. If your child is reading word-by-word, use easier reading material.

For the easiest way to determine a working reading level, use the 'five finger technique.' Ask your child to put down one finger on the page each time a word is unknown. If the book is too hard, five fingers go down right away. This would be at the frustration level.

In order to motivate your child and instill the love of reading, it's really important to use an independent or instructional-leveled book. There can't possibly be any fluency if the book is too hard to begin with. Back to Dewey, capitalize on interests. Interest is more important, probably, than reading level. They just need a lot more help and strategies.

If your child is an older, developing reader, here are more hacks.

1. Read aloud together and to each other, taking turns.
2. Make fun videos reading out loud, especially as a family.
3. Read to another family member or friend.
4. Encourage intonation, emotional reading.

5. Solve any problems such as 'regression' (back skipping).
6. Do Repeated Readings of the same passage to pick up the pace.
7. Use 'Echo Reading.' You whisper read as your child is reading.

As the reader matures, practice rate building activities. Good readers start adapting their rate based on the purpose, why they're reading something. But this takes awhile, so be patient, and start with the basics.

Most important secret of all, if your child is still reading word-by-word and you think you've done it all, go back to the beginning: tracking. Watch how many times your child's eyes stop on a line of print. The more fixations (eye stops), the slower the reading. So increase the 'span' by being aware, lengthening phrases, and reading orally, a lot!

I hope this has been a helpful review of this most interesting topic, reading fluency. I'd love to hear from you.

Every child can improve or enhance fluency, at any level!

Leaving footprints on your reading hearts, Rita

4E

SHOULD STRUGGLING THIRD GRADE READERS BE RETAINED?

October 18, 2015

Just say 'no,' not 'yes' to this.

Today I read that Michigan is pushing for struggling third grade readers to be retained. Other states have also been studying the issue. Obviously by retaining third graders, 4th grade scores will certainly look much improved! But, is that the option we really want? Traditionally, third grade is the cut. Numerous articles have discussed the issue, but please take a look at my commentary.

Third graders need a summer break, not retention.

Data-driven instruction puts a lot of pressure on third graders to be proficient readers. Third grade has traditionally been considered a cut point, meaning until third, students learned to read, kids read to learn, from then on. I do consider that to be true, based on my experience.

However, I have always believed we continue improving our reading all the way through school, and beyond, in adulthood. It's time to reconsider retention as the correct strategy to remediate (or accelerate) children left behind in reading, at any grade level. Instead of the word struggling, let's substitute at-promise. Better yet, scholar-in-waiting.

I am anti-retention in nearly all cases. Here's why:

Supposedly retention gives children the 'gift of time' to catch up and become proficient readers. Truly, in all my years as an educator I cannot recall one case where I thought retention was a viable option.

When I first became a principal, there were actually a couple boys who had been retained twice and they never got better academically because of it. Instead, they were taller, growing facial hair, and generally quite obnoxious in classrooms and on the playground.

I think you will be most interested in our discussion, especially if you have a child considered behind in the fundamental reading skills required by Common Core benchmarks.

Were you aware many states are once again holding kiddos back because their reading is not up to what is considered a currently accepted but arbitrary level?

I find this a poor practice for these valid reasons:

1. Children learn at their own pace, in their own way. There is no timetable.
2. Learning styles may not be considered important in the 'race to the top.'
3. With a 51% poverty rate in public schools, there isn't a level playing field.
4. According to the National Assessment of Educational Progress (NAEP) only 27% of children in the fourth grade are proficient readers.
5. Interventions prior to, or instead of, retention are generally in the child's best interest.
6. Standardized tests may not be reliable, valid, or accurate evaluations of progress.

There are basic building blocks of reading which include:

- Phonemic awareness
- Phonics
- Fluency
- Vocabulary
- Comprehension

Most likely, third graders, (unless ELL, English Language Learners) know the sounds of language. Generally, they have phonics pretty well mastered, but not necessarily. Fundamental phonics includes letter sounds, compound words, prefixes and suffixes, contractions, syllables, etc.

Fluency comments.

First, I am not in favor of any timed test, or using nonsense words of any kind as a gateway to grouping practices. Second, fluency also includes reading with expression at appropriate rates for type of material, and truly, is not about reading a set number of words per minute. Finally, educators generally do not clearly describe fluency in ways we all use the same common language to define it!

Vocabulary.

Frequently vocabulary is taught detached, as separate word lists (not the best idea) or embedded in text. I consider learning vocabulary in context as vastly superior. Reading rich informational, info-text (non-fiction) and literature offers children opportunity to learn new words in context and then use the new words extensively in a wide variety of ways.

Comprehension.

This is the most important skill of all. This is what reading is all about, at its core, or purpose. We read to understand the deep meanings of text and respond to literature. In order to comprehend, children need to know how to preview and review material, ask and answer specific questions, select main ideas and details, summarize and delve deeply into their reading.

Retention: A 'no win,' in most cases.

Age and grade level are very arbitrary in terms of reading achievement. If your child was considered for retention, already held back, or is behind according to 'rigorous' standards in place at your school, I am not surprised—just not happy about it in most situations.

Instead of retention, there are alternatives.

The next obvious question is, what do we do instead of retention? Summer break does not mean a 'brain drain.' Instead, it offers time to relax, then take another look at learning gaps identified by your child's teacher. Of course, you and your child know best what skills could stand a little work.

Set reading goals for the entire family. Go to the library. Use technology. Of most importance, make pleasure reading and mini-skill lessons as important as berry picking and field trips.

Finally, keep the faith. As my friend Don always says, "reading is not rocket science." Anyone can be a coach helping teach a child to read. It's no different than sports. Our kids are all champions in the making when we make the goal reachable and fun along the way.

In fact, let's change the definition here. Instead of calling kids 'struggling readers,' let's call these scholars in waiting, 'at promise readers.'

Leaving footprints on your reading hearts, Rita

4F

DICK AND JANE GO TO KINDERGARTEN. YIKES!
September 25, 2015

What should Kindergartners be expected to know?

I have a big, red, very cool book. It's Ginn's *Dick and Jane Our Big Book*, written in 1948. This book, and most like it in those years, make teaching reading pretty simple. Using a repetition of look-say and some phonics methods, every-day American life looked awesome, if not realistic or practical. Nevertheless, back in the day, kids played simply, like most of these stories, and life in kindergarten was sweeter than sweet.

I remember being in kindergarten more than I would believe. I clearly see my teacher, Miss Welcher. She looked like a teacher back then. Our classroom was loaded with costumes, blocks, rhythm sticks, a piano, and lots and lots to read. That was the norm. We were not expected to know a lot about how to read even though we were, at least, at emergent level. We were learning songs, some letters, playing musical instruments, and swirling and twirling.

What should kindergarteners know about reading?

Dick and Jane taught a lot of kids how to read, even though not every yard had a pony. We've come a long way with rich literature and real life writing.

But there is a chasm between what kindergarteners know and Common Core 'K' Standard, which may surprise you with its rigorous expectations.

There are four major standards in this 'strand.'

Print Concepts, Phonological Awareness, Phonics and Word Recognition. and Fluency. Phew, a lot of skills for kindergarten.

Kindergarten children are my favorite little learners. First they figure out how the classroom works and how to get along with each other. Then learning begins. Kindergarten teachers are unsung heroes and sheroes. Spend a day in kindergarten and you'll know what I mean. Not all kids coming into kindergarten are ready for challenges above their developmental level and that's what's happening now. I worry about teachers' stress as much as the kids.

As a principal I once told our a.m. and p.m. 'K' team I would take their classes so they could do extra planning. At that time, kindergarten teachers lived in a very isolated world. Well, was that brave of me, or? Sixty-four squirrely kids playing 'store,' with fake food and shopping carts flying around! Since I am a firm believer in learning through play, my plans were shattered and my ego took a trouncing. But those two teachers got time together to plan and that's what it was all about. We are now all in the middle of a different, important collegial conversation, involving many stakeholders.

Children are not 'cookie cutter kids.' Common Core standards for kinders.

I am speaking out because kindergarten has become way too academic, with not enough time for fun and being a 'little.' Childhood is a special time! "What's the rush?" is my frequently strong lament. Kindergarten children do not have to know how to read. They are overly assessed already. Scares me.

One size does not fit all, and class size matters. Yet, Common Core expectations are beyond reasonably challenging for kindergarteners and overburdened teachers know what developmentally appropriate practices are. Yet in too many cases they are teaching to meet overly stringent curricula and assessment. Teaching young children is a joy and an art and these talented professionals know best.

What's being taught now.

Of the Common Core 'K Standards: It makes sense to teach basic print concepts, of course. Also, I agree with phonological awareness (sounds of the language). In my opinion, most of the next two levels belong in first grade.

Children who didn't go to preschool may not know how to hold a book, or which way the print goes, following along the line of print, recognizing which way print works, letter sounds and corresponding letters. Big deal, and more so, if the child also wasn't read to at home and didn't visit a library, or have other basic experiences underlying listening, speaking, basic pretend reading, and inventive writing.

It may take awhile to teach that sounds make letters, letters make words, etc. That's why 'language experience' still works for these kids. Writing down children's thinking, experiences, using pictures…then reading it back with help. Isolated skills, not!

Kids drive instruction.

Kindergarten is a time to look for patterns in language, play with manipulatives, savor art, music and motor activities. Play! Learning through play and outdoor education activities, make sense to me. Policy makers need to listen to kindergarten teachers who know best and say good-bye to data-driven instruction. Ask any parent or grandparent. They are a child's first and best teachers.

After my 'Principalship,' I taught with hundreds of kindergarten teachers throughout the U.S. I observed dedicated teachers in print and language rich environments. Recently, in conversations with other teachers, we lamented the loss of rhythm sticks and pianos, replaced by too-early assessment, high level benchmarks, and loss of learning through play.

'Dick and Jane Go to Kindergarten,' not first grade.

Kindergarteners should be pre-readers, learning the sounds of the language and corresponding letters. Kindergarteners are not accomplished readers. The pressure is on so fiercely for children to excel at reading, yet many children are not academically or emotionally ready to pour it on.

Kindergarteners are joyous. Thank you to the multitude of teachers keeping the joy of reading as top priority, regardless of obstacles.

Leaving footprints on your reading hearts, Rita

CHAPTER 5

LITERACY FOR ALL. WHY NOT?
Teacher as a Literacy Champion: Do Kids Have Right to Literacy?

Chapter five extends my essays about reading to the broader topic of 'literacy.' Reading and literacy are not interchangeable, as you find out. Important topics include banned books, world literacy day, right to literacy, national reading test scores and ready–to-use reading recipes for every teacher, parent or coach. Celebrate literacy with 'Read across America.' Get on your party hat! This chapter really packs a wallop.

A) Banned Books Week 2018: When Is Enough, Enough?
B) World Literacy Day 2018: Now What?
C) Do Kids Have a Fundamental Right to Literacy?
D) NAEP 2017 Reading: Up, Down, or Sideways?
E) Little Red Schoolhouse Reading Success Recipes
F) Seussitastical Celebration! Read Across America

5A

BANNED BOOKS WEEK 2018:
WHEN IS ENOUGH, ENOUGH?

September 23, 2018

Celebrate your freedom to read. Read a banned book!

That's right, celebrate your freedom to read! It's an important freedom, and it's protected by the First Amendment. And celebrate the right to read which books we choose. Censorship is censorship. There's a fine line between challenged and banned books. Sometimes it's fine and, sometimes not.

Banned Books Week, promoted by the American Library Association and Amnesty International reminds us freedom is not easily maintained. We must retain our ability to think, reason and have access to thoughts different from our own.

Banned Books Week, Sept. 23-29, 2018, is really about perspective. What you think is offensive, may not offend me, and vice-versa. Who decides? I mean, who decides what we can read, as children, and later, as adults?

Books are still being banned. In 2018. Really! As of this writing, I have not been able to find a simple definitive figure for the number of books challenged and banned this year on the ALA website, which I find disappointing. I don't know the reason.

Well, in truth, the law already decided this very issue. Based on the First Amendment, librarians may not restrict any materials in regard to children, only parents may do so. In Texas v. Johnson, (1989) Justice William J. Brennan gave this opinion:

> *"If there is a bedrock principle underlying the First Amendment, it is that the government may not prohibit the expression of an idea solely because society finds that the idea itself is offensive or disagreeable..."*

In my first year as K-6 school principal, our library clerk came into my office, crying. A well-meaning parent was in the library ripping pages out of books. Back in my office, I counseled them both, and no, books were not to be removed from shelves without proper procedures. Take it to the School Board, fine. But not that day, not in my office. Not with me. Never. And here we are years later, same old stuff. Books being challenged, books being banned.

I taught a number of banned or challenged books during my career as a high school English, Speech, and Reading teacher. Favorites included: *The Giver, Witch of Blackbird Pond, To Kill a Mocking Bird, Bridge to Terabithia, Tuck Everlasting, Lord of the Flies.*

I don't know about you, but I want to read what I want to read. Everybody has different tastes, I know, but there's plenty to read to suit everybody's preferences. That's what we're really talking about, isn't it? Preferences.

Well, I prefer not to have anyone tell me what I can or cannot read. Looking at today's list of most frequently challenged books, I do see commonalities. To me, anything having to do with currently-in-vogue morals and values, juxtaposed with a to- frequently divisive landscape is on the list. Stuff we need to read to understand one another, to know. Let's look.

Top ten most frequently challenged books of 2017

1. *Thirteen Reasons Why*, Jay Asher (suicide discussion).
2. *The Absolute True Diary of a Part Time Indian*, Sherman Alexie (profanity, sex)
3. *Drama*, Raina Telgemeier (LGBT, etc.)
4. *The Kite Runner*, Khaled Hosseini (Islamic questions)
5. *George*, Alex Gino (transgender child)
6. *Sex is a Funny Word;* Cory Silverberg (sex education, etc.)
7. *To Kill a Mockingbird*, Harper Lee (violence, use of 'N' word)
8. *The Hate U Give*, Angie Thomas (drugs, profanity, vulgar)
9. *And Tango Makes Three*, Parnell and Richardson (same-sex relationship)
10. *I Am Jazz*, Herthel and Jennings (gender identity)

I didn't intend to write a blog today, but it's our 'Family Weekend' and I've promised to be fully present, not blogging. But there it was, this topic, so darn juicy, so relevant for today, staring me right in the face. My family talked about this, we agreed it was important to discuss, together, as one, and hope our readers will spend time talking about it at the schoolhouse, business, and home.

We are all affected, not just librarians taking unwanted criticism. Teachers, Principals, School Boards, County Offices, and possibly Courts, may be the ultimate deciders in what books are read in classrooms and school libraries. It's a huge business. Follow the money. Really not knowledgeable what happens in public libraries, in regard to books being challenged and banned. I intend to get more information now. I'm sure it's an issue.

I can tell you this. I have been working on this blog topic for a couple days now, and there is so much more I want to learn, including challenges and bans. Numbers, types, procedures, remedies, locations, etc. Who is really in charge of what we read? Aren't we?

Our Eugene Public Library is so impressive, it was their Banned Books Week Campaign that inspired me to write this article for us to think about. Banned Book Week is no Dr. Seuss party week. However, it is, in one broad sweep a tremendous undertaking, to protect the reading and writing rights of all people.

I thank the American Library Association and local libraries for encouraging the protection of people who write thought-provoking, relevant titles. It is imperative that authors are free from persecution or threat from others thinking differently.

This is my third recent article as a triple header of literacy stories. "World Literacy Day 2018: Now What?" and "Do Kids Have a Fundamental Right to Literacy?" Now this. Get people literate, then let them read!

Morgan said "It is not fair. Anyone can read what she or he wants to read. Even if someone says you can or can't, you can read it, because you want to read it. I just need permission from my mom and dad to say I can read it. Other people don't get to tell me what I can or can't read."

Pretty profound for a seven-year old, second grader. She had been listening to our grown up discussion, which was most interesting.

Did you know *The Wizard of Oz* was a banned book for a number of years? I was surprised to read that! There are so many books that have been censored over the years. What titles would you add to our ever-growing list?

Children's books and young adult fiction are also frequently challenged. From ALA (American Library Association) comes another list. It even includes picture books. Really.

Challenged kids' list

1. *I Am Jazz*, Herthel and Jennings (transgender child)
2. *The Watsons Go to Birmingham*, Paul Curtis (offensive language, etc.)
3. *Where's Waldo*, Martin Hanford (beach scene)

4. *Baseball Saved Us*, Ken Mochizuki (internment camps, racial slur)
5. *Anastasia Krupnik*, Lois Lowry (teen life, drinking, sex, etc.)
6. *It's a Girl Thing, How to Stay Healthy, Safe, and in Charge*, Mavis Jukes (puberty)

Can you imagine, *Where's Waldo?* Better go grab my two copies from Morgan's library shelves. It's supposed to show people on the beach. In particular, a version published in 1987 apparently showed a glimpse of a woman's bare top, and somebody spotted it, I certainly never would have. I can barely find Waldo. I am clueless, other than that one sketch, why this book would be challenged.

It's more important than ever for us to encourage and support an educated electorate. Many children and adults still do not have access to public or school libraries and internet access. Our libraries serve a critical function. Everyone deserves the right to read whatever perceived of interest or benefit. Nobody should be told what to read. Or what should not be read. Never. No Censorship!

This topic remains a work in progress.

Banned Book Week, couple of ideas.

First, join together as a collective voice and say, "No!" to censorship. Period. Next, know what procedures are in place for challenging, or actually getting a book banned. Also, support public and school libraries. Fully staff and fund our libraries. Finally, maintain relevant, current titles wanted and needed by a literate, interested community with the right, by law, to know!

Look, I understand this is a really tough, tough topic for us. In fact, a book was read last year in first grade I thought was really gross and inappropriate for that grade level. As a nana, I kept silent. But now I wonder what procedures are in place for a parent concerned about a particular book being read or taught in the classroom? Or on a classroom or library shelf?

So I see all sides of this issue, with many perspectives, different combinations and permutations, for sure. What do you think?

Leaving footprints on your reading hearts, Rita

5B

WORLD LITERACY DAY 2018: NOW WHAT?

September 8, 2018

THIS: I read that 775 million adults lack minimum literacy skills.

One-in-five adults, two thirds of them are women. Not so bad—or staggering—depending on our perspective. Sobering, 60.7 million children are out of school and more drop out. Is this acceptable? As a nation of readers, we believe that 'the joy of reading is a joy forever.' But we know, at a minimum, that reading generally leads to better jobs and the ability to cope with an ever changing political and social environment.

There are several types of literacy; perhaps we are considering math, science, and other disciplines. For my purposes here, let's stay with the notion of 'literacy' as being able to read, write, and master basic language needed for daily life.

Today, September 8th is International Literacy Day, or World Literacy Day. In 1966 United Nations Educational Scientific and Cultural Organization (UNESCO) designated Sept. 8th each year as International Literacy Day, focusing on literacy for all. First celebrated in 1967, the day highlights the need for literacy in many facets of daily life.

Fifty-two years later, not much has changed. This year's theme, 'Literacy and Skills Development' is particularly significant, I think with our renewed emphasis on global networking. The world grows smaller as we acknowledge our interdependence.

Most likely there is a connection between countries with high levels of poverty and illiteracy. Women typically severely bear the brunt of a lack of education. It seems so overwhelming; we must tackle this together, as one united worldwide people.

The issue of illiteracy and literacy is also on the forefront of the United Nations' 'Sustainable Development Goals.' This is a monumental, heroic undertaking. I fully support this endeavor, and I'm sure you do too.

However, Literacy Day actually casts a wider net, celebrating advances as well as needs that remain in math, digital competency, technical skills, and softer skills needed for success in today's rapidly changing economy and the everyday world of work.

Goals developed by world leaders in 2015, clearly define tackling universal access to schooling and lifelong learning opportunities. *"The day focuses on skills and competencies required for employment, careers and livelihoods, particularly technical and vocational skills, along with transferable skills and digital skills."*

No this is not Dr. Seuss day. I am not suggesting we put on party hats. But in order to get to a Seussitastical Celebration, kiddos need to know how to read and write, of course. I recently wrote about the Michigan legal case where the judge said "No, literacy is not, by our Constitution, a fundamental student right." Shocking. I so disagree.

As a reading teacher for more than forty years, I taught in every conceivable classroom, at all levels, homeschoolers, adults, credential students, etc. Literacy has been my cause and hopefully, my legacy will be strong. Because of my background, today is especially important in my life as educator.

In order to see where we were then and where we are now headed, let's review recent NAEP (National Assessment of Educational Progress) scores. Our Nation's Report Card, this snapshot glance at reading, tells us since 1992 there has been a slight gain in reading scores, maybe about five or so points at the 4th and 8th grade levels, but scores are generally flat. NAEP is one of the few assessments I trust, as I consider it to be valid and reliable.

Minority children showed depressing scores at mostly basic levels of under 18th percentiles. We have to do better. Despite No Child Left Behind, Common Core and accompanying educational innovations, learning gaps are in some cases larger than ever, and the playing fields have not been leveled as we hoped.

What can we do now?

That is the central question. As a nation of servant leaders and optimists, the answer is not to just work harder. It's easy to say build capacity in our organizations while working lean, following tenets of business as our guide.

It's also one thing to write continuously about growth mindset, grit, mindfulness, kindness, and love. I do it too. I write about stuff that is pretty fluffy and sweet, but not getting the whole job done, maybe. Soft skills are so necessary in our rapidly thrusting future is now, today life.

But harder, must-have fundamental skills are also my roadmap and recipe for success. Just as much. With all the emphasis on achievement and money poured into testing companies, where did all the money go since 1992? Good question. Easy answer: it just did. Flat scores? Show us the money! Not tied with tests that are not reliable and valid in many instances, or useful to teachers and schools.

Looking closer to home, what do I think needs to happen to give all kids a fair chance at literacy? I hope to see this happen in my lifetime; why not do the following things now?

1. Fully fund public schools. That means everything. Adequate school buildings, supplies, materials, tech, and texts. Everything.

2. Stop the incessant testing madness. Re-think use of Data Points and Data Walls.
3. Pay teachers fairly. Teachers work year 'round, constantly.
4. Every school needs a functional library and librarian.
5. Literacy is a school-wide emphasis, with integrated curriculum and celebrations.
6. Create a culture of reading that invites children to want to read both fiction and info-text.
7. Plan for lots of time for fun reading and take the fear out of reading, as timed tests.
8. Home school partnerships and business partnerships are so rewarding.

It is cruel and unfortunate that because of poor reading skills, many students are unable to access or be successful in rigorous core curriculums. Perhaps we might question the efficacy of these curriculums in terms of balance, energy, interest, cost and effectiveness.

We need to take another look at how we teach writing, in combination with reading, to promote the needed balance, literate readers and writers. To do this, teachers need more time for collaboration, collegial conversation, a chance to team or co-teach.

Professional development must include time to talk, listen, learn, demonstrate for one another and share best practices. Teachers are action researchers each and every day. So let's listen, really listen and make adjustments, mid-course corrections to get where we need to go, for the kids' sake.

Our young scholars in waiting need us to cut to the chase, to dump what's not working for us, and them. We must be risk-takers and plan-makers. To share best practices and classroom-tested and perfected reading lessons, cross content, all grade levels. Not just K-3. What is our Vision and Mission, in regard to literacy?

Start with our budding preschoolers, modeling the joy of reading and the fundamental skills necessary to start the journey to literacy and beyond. We learn to read, then read to learn, it's true. Kids still need to know how to read, read better, faster, so that means all levels, through adult. A big job to do, but, oh, such a pleasure getting there.

Schools and families participating in a seamless effort between school and home, what a combo. 'Parents Are Our Partners' and a child's first and best teachers. Better together. Reading to toddlers? Extend way past that, and read together more than the minimum twenty minutes a day.

A final thought.

What is needed is a larger global effort to get all children to school, provide literacy instruction, and technology. A massive undertaking, but achievable.

As a nation of literate and fair-minded people, we can help UNESCO and the United Nations achieve their admirable goals. By being connected with other like-minded educators and stakeholders, sharing best governmental programs and teacher practices, we are off to a good start.

Local libraries also need our support to ensure digital and text access for all children. Moreover, we need to figure out better ways to get kiddos to and from local afterschool programs and resources. Kids may be living in cars or shelters but those cars are probably not headed to a library. Gas costs money. And please, no more libraries closing and librarians cut out of budgets. We need both.

We cannot afford to do less. We must to do more. Hungry children cannot learn. So start with Maslow, add in Dewey, the rest up to us. We make the difference in the literacy lives of countless children, here in America and across the world.

Leaving footprints on your reading hearts, Rita

5C

DO KIDS HAVE A FUNDAMENTAL RIGHT TO LITERACY?
July 7, 2018

The Judge Ruled 'NO!'

Michigan Judge Stephen Murphy III recently ruled children do not have a fundamental right to learn to read and write. This long lasting, far reaching decision responded to a lawsuit filed in 2016 by Public Counsel, for plaintiffs, students in five of Detroit's most poorly performing schools, including public and charter.

The case was called *Gary B. v. Snyder.* It named, among others, Governor Snyder, Michigan Board of Education etc. The 136-page complaint, highlighted need for literacy and adequate education for all Detroit schoolchildren, as well as remedies for lack of appropriate facilities, class sizes, learning conditions and access to the proverbial level playing field for beleaguered students.

I really don't know where to start or what to say. It is so disheartening to read the backstory of the Michigan Judge's decision that children don't have a fundamental right to literacy.

I saw the story on Twitter about a week ago, have been knocking it around in my head until I found a day to cocoon, do significant research and then write what I think. So that is exactly where I am and not really happy about it. It's just stuck in my head and heart.

I find it so ironic after forty-six years as a reading teacher at every conceivable level, I am compelled to define or defend why children must be literate. I do consider it a fundamental right of every child to learn to read and write. We are a nation of more than writing an x as a signature. We are better than that.

I spent most of today in fervent discussion about the various issues and ramifications of the original lawsuit, with my California colleague and longtime writing partner, Don Werve.

We batted around each article, hitting the mother lode with the original one hundred thirty-six page plaintiff complaint, *Gary B. v Snyder*. Don's opinion ended with the question: "Is literacy as fundamental right under law or moral responsibility of a civilized society?" Beginning with children attending school, our grandchildren deserve the legacy of literacy and joy of reading.

So, having to start somewhere...

Let's start with the role of compulsory education. In the United States we have traditionally mandated Compulsory Education. While Principal I participated in Homeless Coalition, Literacy Boards and most significant, SARB, School Attendance and Review Board. 'You Miss School, You Miss Out.'

It was our task to get kiddos to school, no matter what. I was still in California then, and it was law that children attend school. Parents or guardians of truant kids ultimately could be arrested.

Today all states still have compulsory education on the books, had at least since 1918, and I find no significant changes. Michigan's law states that children must attend school full time, from six to eighteen and the law has been law since 1871. A long time. Compulsory education is one big piece of the lawsuit pie.

Detroit's school teachers have for too long tolerated gross working conditions, with reports of books dating back to 1998, rats and other unsanitary conditions, lack of resources, large class sizes. Schools were placed under State control about in 1999, so to me, this mess goes right to the state who took over the school districts. They are responsible.

With quality schools, young scholars would have access to technology, a chance to excel. Watch those scores climb and skills grow. Literate kids ready to contribute to society.

I read where Governor Snyder acknowledged many of the Detroit issues, but I found few or no remedies.

The State of Michigan, where I was born, ranked last in a snapshot of forty three states in reading proficiency for African American children on a recent sampling from NAEP, our Nation's Report Card.

The five poorly performing schools in the lawsuit were indeed underperforming. According to NAEP, (National Assessment of Educational Progress), in 2015, these Detroit schools underperformed to the tune of last in rank of big city schools in reading and math. Fourth grade African American children were 91% below proficiency in reading and math.

Michigan and retentions.

Three years ago I wrote a blog post about Michigan wanting to retain all third grade students not meeting standards in reading. That is happening in 2019-20 school year!

So excuse me, I am confused here. Literacy is or isn't important? Important to make children go to school, important to read at or above grade level to a proficiency, but not a right to do so? My head is spinning.

Ok, so let's put a couple pieces together. We know from witness accounts, hearing from teachers and Governor statements that many schools in Detroit are grossly substandard in every way.

Children cannot participate in a democratic society or find meaningful work without the ability to at least read and write, much less do math. How does that happen in such substandard schools?

Must schools provide the children's basic education in literacy? Is it a fundamental right? Should they learn these basic skills at home, or as part of home school, of some configuration, in lieu of public school?

What public schools do.

Schools are supposed to teach students how to read and write. What is the bare bones minimum? Is this a fundamental right, or not? Do children have a right to literacy, or not? The complaint lines out in great detail why literacy is critical and how it is a basic right for all children. The Judge did not agree.

I understand why the Judge ruled the way he did, although it causes reflection and great angst knowing no bounds. I am sure he took the strict, narrow wording, and conceptual approach that the Constitution or Bill or Rights did not specifically include literacy. Therefore, no fundamental right delineated, no fundamental right—no matter how important literacy actually is to our democratic society.

Interesting in the forty-page opinion, literacy was mentioned as a necessary facet of American life. However, by staying with the strict constitutional interpretation, no fundamental right is guaranteed. So the Judge may be right by a slim interpretation, most narrow indeed. The ramifications are a heartbreaker.

I suspect the ruling will go to the Sixth Court of Appeals and ultimately to the Supreme Court. Since the case was filed in 2016, I would surmise this case will go on for a long time and the outcome, one can only guess, with political considerations and a changing Supreme Court.

Educators, Board members, parents all have a vested interest in this decision. Do we, as a nation of readers and learners, believe our children have a fundamental right to learn to read and write? If so, who is to meet that right, the schoolhouse or home? Or...?

If schools are to continue providing world-class education, funding must take a priority, testing must cease and as a collective voice we stand and say "enough!" Our children are precious; our schools must be top notch. Young scholars can't be tech-savvy without the fundamental building blocks of literacy. How's that future ready curriculum looking without commitment to literacy as the backbone?

And most significant, what kind of message has been given to educators striving to provide excellence in instruction, overcoming all odds? What message is given our parents, and society as a whole, about the lack of importance of literacy?

It's one thing to acknowledge literacy has meaning and significance. It's another to be right, to the letter of the law. Maybe, since I am not a lawyer, but in this court of public opinion, let's take a vote.

Leaving footprints on your reading hearts, Rita

5D

NAEP 2017 Reading: Up, Down or Sideways?
April 10, 2018

Don't show mama our nation's report card! Not so good.

Tonight I'm sharing my opinions, not a major statistical treatise, but I will toss some information into the bowl, like *Strega Nona*, and let's mix it up, and put a little honey on top.

Tonight I offer heartfelt, plain talk about yesterday's shocking headlines, or not so, really, that our kids have failed. Or at least, didn't show any growth in fourth and eighth grade reading. Goodness. Yet here we are in America, right in the middle of endless standardized testing.

Now this. Drat. Flat scores. The sideways. Up scores, like Florida. Down, like second language learners and special needs-labeled students.

I am genuinely concerned. Policymakers better not even breathe in the direction of charters or private sector takeover as overreaction. Our public schools, already significantly overwhelmed, often under siege and under supported, starved in many cases, years of neglect, emotionally and financially. But let's not go there, not now, not tonight.

About the NAEP exams.

NAEP (National Assessment of Educational Progress) has traditionally been considered a valid indicator of educational progress. It uses a statistically large sample and has consistently been fair and to the point. NAEP offers us a snapshot of what's happening with children's academic progress. Until now. We seriously need to look at the validity and reliability of the 2017 exams.

About assessment.

To be effective, assessment for teachers, parents and kids, it has to be useful.

To be effective, assessment for teachers, parents and kids, it has to be reliable and valid.

To be effective, assessment for teachers, parents and kids, it has to be immediate.

It's critically important for any standardized test, however large the sample, to be reliable over a long enough period to track, or show a trend. It was, definitely through 2015, the last real growth in reading, although nothing to brag about.

To be valid, an assessment measures the same thing the same way. This year's test scores are like comparing the proverbial apples with oranges. I understand NAEP, after fifteen years exploration and study wanted to go completely digital, of course, only makes sense.

This year NAEP was given part and part. Eighty percent of kiddos took the tests digitally, twenty percent, traditional pencil and paper. A valid sample size of 585,000 kids participated. That gives credence without going any further. A lot of kids involved, therefore a lot of information.

At what price did our nation's students sacrifice accurate rendering of what they know, because of the stress and newness of the test methodology? NAEP, in comparative research studies determined no significant difference, or improved scores digitally, but I'm really not sure.

This is a difficult question, as our children are generally whizzes at technology and most probably are routinely tested via tech apps and assessments, but who knows?

Regardless, until the next assessments in a couple years, with all children taking the test digitally, one wonders. States where children's scores declined are most definitely looking at this factor.

Of course I am not sure, but I bet the delays in releasing the scores, originally expected in October, were to ensure the data is in fact, accurate, maybe even to prepare for anticipated criticism. I read that NAEP thoroughly reviewed the matter to reassure us.

So that being said, let's look at just the big picture of the new results, assuming accuracy in data. Truthfully, when the NAEP tests wholly on digital, that should start a new trend line, as it did from 1992. I doubt this will happen.

Looking at the scores.

Only about one-third of our children in eighth grade read at or near proficient level. Worse, the achievement gap widened. Flat scores for most children, most states, with few noteworthy exceptions, as Florida, where scores went up in fourth and eighth, including subgroups.

Here we go again. You saw the classroom pictures. You heard about second jobs. You heard about teachers crying at soup kitchens. Pretty sad. Now hold those same teachers accountable? Blame game? Fully fund public schools. End the testing madness. Put the money into fair salaries and classrooms. Lower class sizes. Watch what happens to these scores.

Was it this test? Can it be true after all these years of reforms that only one-third of America's fourth and eighth graders read at proficient levels? Why? We know how to teach reading.

Our NAEP Report card shows mostly a 'C,' flat scores, mostly sideways, a little up and down. Not much. And that is the problem, my colleagues, parents, and friends. No big growth.

Title I came about in 1965, under President Lyndon Johnson. Its stated goal was to bring all children, equally to educational parity. All children. After many years of ESEA Title I. After No Child Left Behind. After ESSA.

Achievement gap widened.

The gap widened in these just released scores. It was supposed to narrow, then go away. Didn't happen, gap worsened. For special needs children and ELL, second language learners who probably shouldn't be tested anyway, scores went down.

As I said, the intent of the original Title I legislation was to narrow the achievement gap. When you read NAEP statistics you notice that scores did go up steadily from 1992 to 2003. Since then, scores reflect a spotty situation. There are some highs and some very lows. The biggest problem I see in this last blast of scores is that the highest achieving group of children, the upper twenty-five percent carried modest if any gains at all on the reading tests.

Flat scores.

Let me repeat, really no change at all for fourth and eighth reading. The extremely minor eighth grade one point gain, to 267 on a 500 point score in reading, since 2015, was not equally distributed. The lower achieving children did not raise their scores, they dropped. Disturbing trend, if it is a trend. I'm not sure yet.

With teacher strikes as a backdrop, NAEP 2017 dropped the bad news yesterday.

Tonight I am referring only to reading, as that is my area of expertise. Math scores, however, were about the same, across the board, generally flat.

Standardized testing is a conundrum.

So much emphasis, to the detriment of class activities. Teaching to the test. Loss of curricular programs, needed way more than practice tests and endless hours of assessment. Numbing.

The pendulum boat definitely needs to be rocked. And now this. These scores. Exactly.

Education Week, a leading professional publication, reported grim results. "Average scores for most states remained unchanged from 2015 in either grade or subject and more states saw declines than improvements." The article also pointed to widening gaps, stating, "Low-achieving students are declining."

Between 1992 and 2015, NAEP reading scores increased by six points at grade-four and five points at grade-eight. Fourth grade was not statistically different than 2013. In eighth grade reading, these results were lower than 2013. Disturbing!

In February 2016, I wrote my first NAEP blog post for BAM Radio Network EdWords, "Been Down So Long Looks Like Up to Me." I didn't think the scores could be lower, I expected an upward spurt this time. Not so. And, sadly, it was no surprise that black and Hispanic children scored even lower than the other children.

Since these scores remained the same, or in some cases dropped further, the only way to go is up. We have a common ground, a starting place to figure out where we are as a nation of readers, and where to go from here.

Tonight, call me hopeful. Our goal remains to help make every child a reader. That is, a capable confident reader in a nation of readers. Reading is a joy forever! World-class scholars are in the making. We are the ones to do it. Now! Finland is often regarded as a gold class standard in literacy, but we are every bit as good, maybe better.

Leaving footprints on your reading hearts, Rita

5E

LITTLE RED SCHOOLHOUSE READING SUCCESS RECIPES
April 9, 2016

One room schoolhouse.

It seemed so simple back then. One room, a bunch of kids all learning together. Teaching each other. Pretty much the same today, don't you think? Right now, close your eyes, imagine what it would be like to teach in a no-technology-based one-room schoolhouse, with kiddos of all ages and stages. We've come a long way. The best is yet to be.

Tonight I am positive we are turning the corner in American education. In particular, you know I am most concerned about reading and literacy. You are all the technology experts. I still have my Mac tutor. But what I know is reading, so I like to model literacy topics.

For many years I studied champions in all walks of life. I wanted to know how did they get in the flow state, stay in the zone and continually roll like smooth operators in the bigger outside world? By teaching with so many teachers it really improved my practices, and my Spanish, a little. I saw a lot of kids in the highest state of learning, the optimum way to learn anything. It seems learning states go like this: On task, engaged, flow. Now I see a lot of engaged and flow state kids on Social Media without having to travel. What a gift.

Things are different now.

I think American educators, really all educators, worldwide are talking about some basic things.

- Grit and mindsets. (Resilience and self-esteem?)
- Importance of play and recess
- Ditch texts or keep?
- Homework, 'yay' or 'nay?'
- What about all those darn tests?
- How to group, re-group & differentiate instruction?
- Best ways to integrate technology & traditional instruction?
- Catch "gap kids" up in basic skills.
- Do the mandates, yet keep the creative juices flowing.
- Keep up with minute-to-minute changes in our fast-paced world.
- Model the joy of learning, and the love of reading.
- How to organize a learning setting, for flexible uses.
- Of course, more.

I admit, the NAEP (National Assessment of Educational Progress) reading scores unglued me. I worry about tired teachers, kid-worthy use of instructional time, one hundred thirteen tests, getting back on track exploring a world of new adventures through reading, a combination of classic and trendy literature and non-fiction. Balance.

Reading needs to be a top priority. The hands-on activities, PBL (Project Based Learning), technology projects, maker spaces. I appreciate them all and see their value. However, the basic foundational skills are at the cornerstone of any project. I think that reading is part of literacy, but now believe there can be literacy without reading, and I am so reluctant to see that.

About and literacy.

- Recognizing there are many kids who benefit from a mentor, all K-12 teachers must be reading interventionists. There are kids in every class needing a boost in basic skills.
- Everybody needs to know how to teach reading, cross content areas. There are reading skills particular to every subject.
- Think about this: How do you model reading & literacy?
- What is reading, really?
- What is literacy?
- Difference between reading and literacy?

I happen to have a 1936 *Readers Digest,* featuring an article "Americans Can't Read." This is hard to imagine. All the way back then. In 1967, Jeanne Chall wrote *Learning To Read, The Great Debate.*

There are many more outstanding reading researchers and teachers who told us stories. Time-tested, classroom-perfected reading strategies are important to share. So here's what I think we should consider to replicate awesome programs going in America's schools right now, especially for reading improvement. All kids can read better, faster and savor reading. All levels. Here goes:

'Big Idea' reading program hacks.

- Increase amount of collegial conversation about best practices, K-12.
- Give teachers autonomy re program, strategies, assessment and best use of resources.
- Rethink school-wide reading incentive programs.
- Do SSR (Sustained Silent reading) or DEAR (Drop Everything And Read) school-wide.
- Read out loud to your class every day, regardless of grade level.
- Give kids time to read, whether graphic novels, any choice selection, at independent level.

- Have a reading mentor. Share ideas. Co-teach your classes.
- Invite your Principal, parents and other community members to participate in reading fun!
- Revisit basic reading skills in phonics, vocabulary, comprehension and practice fluency.
- Involve parents and community in a wide variety of school and home activities and partnerships.

Back in 1960, Russell Stauffer first described 'Directed Reading Activities,' which suggested metacognition—awareness of one's own thought process—is vital in 'explicit strategy instruction.' Because of the need for reading intervention for some students today, DRA's are more significant than ever.

We know that skillful readers are very strategic when they read, so we do previewing and overviewing, close reading, summarizing, and rehearsing. Teachers who instruct by explaining, then modeling appropriate strategies, engage in what researcher Pressley termed 'transactional strategies instruction' because the strategies highlighted students' relationships and interactions with text.

Fostering the joy of lifelong reading is the heart and soul of every reading program. Great literature connects us with life experiences, interesting characters, places and times. By using a mixture of junior novels with high interest literature, significant literary heritage is continued by a new generation of recreational readers.

Finally, I believe teachers could easily manage that one room schoolhouse, potbelly stove and all, as long as their capes don't get too close.

Leaving footprints on your reading hearts, Rita

5F

Birthdays are always special.

When it's time to party for Dr. Seuss, it's a big hurray for the day! Mark your calendar-March 2nd. Happy birthday, Dr. Seuss! And get set for the party of parties, Read Across America!

Two of my grandkids have Valentine birthdays. One, a teenager, amazes me with her accomplishments: band, AP classes, Scouts, you name it. The years just flew by and birthday parties for her are not about pin the tail anymore.

Morgan, our Eugene adorable, is turning six. Our kindergartener is debating between various character themes, but it's going to be an old fashioned, at home party this year and we're pretty excited about that. This is our year of simple is best. Trips to the Dollar Store already, need a head start on a 'big girl' party, complete with party dress and maybe a little lip gloss. Bet she invites Carter, planning to marry him.

Our kinder party prep is small potatoes compared to the across America planning going on right now for the gala annual Dr. Seuss event. No matter how big or small, it's a perfect time to look at the collections of a many hued and nuanced Dr. Seuss. I'll bet you find a couple new to you. Always happens to me.

Read Across America.

There is a really big Seussitastical celebration coming up, time to get ready for the party of parties! Read Across America, a signature project of the National Education Association, is a great uniter. This year, I think we all need a grand adventurous, light-hearted party hat of party hats. Don't you agree?

March 2nd each year, the NEA, National Education Association honors Dr. Seuss big time on his birthday. And what a fun literacy fiesta it is! You're all set with ready-to-go lesson plans, event organization, city visit schedule, press releases, etc. One click on NEA Read Across America and a multitude of resources awaits you.

First celebrated in 1998, this is the annual frosting on the literacy cake, perfect party for school and home, all ages and stages. I can't think of anything better.

Last year there was an unexpected addition to Dr. Seuss' prolific collection, *What Pet Should I Get?* Found in a box, the missed manuscript offers a glorious story. Perhaps there will be more to come, who knows?

I love classic Dr. Seuss books. Each one is filled with colorful, creative, magical, really cool characters and settings. The fabulous illustrations are exciting for children and stimulate interesting conversation, art, music, and writing. Actually, thinking about Oobleck, I'm sure we can combine and connect with many thematic, blended learning activities.

Dr. Seuss was a prolific writer.

Did you realize Dr. Seuss (Theodor Geisel) wrote forty six books? I know about half of them really well and keep discovering new favorites. Independent bookstores offer a great source of offbeat titles we may have missed, so take a peek. Thank you Dr. Seuss for making us smile, fingers snapping and toes tapping to your magical, lyrical beat!

Here are some reasons we love your work so much, and remind ourselves that play is learning. Your stories are heartwarming, instructional, and help build fluency.

Hacks for teaching Dr. Seuss:

1. Use sing-song voices.
2. Experiment with language patterns.
3. Learn through concrete play (manipulate letters).
4. Teach basic phonemic awareness and phonics (sounds and letters).
5. Read out loud, together, varying rate and expression.
6. Practice counting and basic math.
7. The descriptive language is strong.
8. Rhyme, rhythm and predictable patterns make sense to new readers (hop on pop).
9. Perfect for all ages (he even wrote for adults).
10. Great for struggling readers, new language learners, special needs.

Playful language patterns, tongue twisters and innovative language inventions make reading a grand adventure. Simple poetry, a lyrical beat makes reading a treat! Get out those rhythm instruments, start moving and grooving!

I've never met anyone who didn't like these adventurous stories and unique worlds. What's more fun than using puppets, props or wearing silly hats and costumes? Better yet, each Dr. Seuss book offers teaching opportunities connecting themes and units, and various basic skills. This includes weather, counting, alphabet, phonemic awareness, phonics such as' word families' (at, cat, sat, etc.), rhyme, rhythm and predictable patterns. Amazing!

When I am with my family, there is always a lot of Dr. Seuss being read. In December Morgan and I read *How The Grinch Stole Christmas*, Jan. featured *The Tooth Book*. (Oh that first lost tooth!) February all set with *Happy Birthday to You*. Our ready-to-read pile also includes: *The Sneetches, The Cat's Quizzer, The Lorax, There's a Wocket in My Pocket*, and *Oh Say, Can You Say, What's the Weather Today?*" Varied reading levels.

Morgan and I read *Butter Battle* which I blogged about earlier, because getting along is for everyone.

I love these books. Wear your Seuss party hat and fill your party bag with this sampler:

1. *Bartholomew and the Oobleck*: Seasons, weather, sequence, scientific method, science experiment. Vocabulary.
2. *I Can Read with My Eyes Shut*: Colors, syllables, spelling (Mississippi), contractions, rhyming.
3. *The Cat in the Hat*: Word families (ay, at, out; ake, an, ot). Rhyme and repetition.
4. *Dr. Seuss' ABC*: Alphabet (Upper and lower case letters), rhyming, colors, predictable patterns.
5. *Hop On Pop*: Simple Dr. Seuss. Few words on each page. Rhyming. Word families (ed, all, op, ing, op, own, ee, ad, at). Also concepts of mother, father, sister and brother.
6. *One Fish, Two Fish, Red Fish, Blue Fish*: Opposites, direction, counting, word families.
7. *Green Eggs and Ham*: Rhythm, rhyme, word families, predictable patterns.
8. *Ten Apples on Top*: Great counting book, Seuss-style. Abacus handy? Apples!
9. *Oh, the Places You'll Go!*: Directions, rhyming, motivational for everybody!

I know we all savor the words and colorful tip-of-the tongue language in these wonderful stories. Sharing Dr. Seuss is a special class and family time tradition all year long, not just on his birthday.

One last title to highlight, the newest, *What Pet Should I Get?* This manuscript was literally found in a box. Written more than fifty years ago, Dr. Seuss' love of animals shines brightly in the story and is still timely.

Mini Lesson: *What Pet Should I Get?*

1. Read straight through as a Read-Aloud.
2. Do a Book Walk: Check out the front, back covers and illustrations.
3. Background knowledge ('schema'): Do you have a pet at home? If so what? Who takes care of the pet? Who picked the pet? Etc.
4. Looking at the front and back book covers, make predictions what the book is going to be about. Count how many pets are on the front cover and name them.
5. What is the strange looking pet on the back cover?
6. Listen for repeating rhymes. "We want a pet. We want a pet. What kind of pet should we get?" Look for word families: ing, ish, all, etc, etc.

What a grand ending. What a pet!

And now for the ending. SHHHH I'll whisper it to you. Did you hear it? Ask your kiddos to write, draw, retell parts of the story, favorite characters, pets, and the best one ye: Which pet DID Dr. Seuss pick? Did you like the ending? Were you surprised? I was!

I'd love to hear about your favorite Dr. Seuss' titles and your very special 'Read Across America.' No, I didn't forget Horton!

Leaving footprints on your reading hearts, Rita

CHAPTER 6

Preschool, Teaching Littlest Learners

Teacher as a Lifelong Learner:
Making a Case for Universal Preschool.

Chapter six is sure to bring a smile to your face and a joyous moment or two in every missive. Everybody is a teacher, one way or another. But not everyone can be a great preschool teacher. I surely found that out! Enjoy my preschool adventures. Chapters one-through-four tell you quite a bit about me, but the sweet stories in this chapter reveal my growth as a teacher of youngest children. Preschool, for me, is a world of tiny kiddos learning emergent reading skills, during busy days filled with washing hands, outdoor play, sharing, and caring.

A) Universal Preschool: Bliss-Worthy!
B) Learning to Read, Covered with Jello, Bugs and Snails
C) Learning to Teach Littlest Angels, Life Lessons for All
D) Did You Bring Seaweed Salad Today, Rita?
E) Let's Start at the Very Beginning!
F) Teaching Littlest Kids to Read…Or Not?
G) Life Lessons from 'Littles'

6A

UNIVERSAL PRESCHOOL: BLISS-WORTHY!

July 22, 2016

I love teaching every grade level!

Each is unique and has its own challenges. At the moment I am focusing my attention to preschool. The kids are simply a riot and if you need a jolt of joy, join the fun.

What if: Preschool for all?

Tonight I'm sharing my thoughts with you about the importance of universal preschool. In reality, probably that's not starting soon enough, brain-wise. We really need to be focusing at least birth-through-two or three. Let's just agree on preschool as a starting point.

Preschools are a mixed bag, ranging from day care to full-on fantastic learning experiences, it just depends.

Our 'flowers' need early nurturing. We can help. Fund, respect, align with kindergarten skills, pay teachers fairly. Volunteer. Legislative efforts. Start a dialogue regarding the tremendous value of earlier childhood education. Really promote the children's organizations you already support.

I was dismayed to read our country is way behind most other countries in educational funding for these critical learning years. Why?

How do we know what to teach preschoolers when the world is turning upside down? Information is zooming at us at light speed; perhaps we need to rethink the purpose of schooling and where we go next. What skills and attributes will kids really need to know to thrive in a new, constantly changing economy and life?

Paying attention to value of early education.

What does make sense to me is starting really early with kids. Expose each child to print and language-rich experiences, as well as appropriate technology. Ensure a seamless path from home to school, and understand many stakeholders do care enough to invest in early childhood education as a cause.

Start learning early, in a schoolhouse way; it just makes good sense. I am aware public schools are already underfunded, of course. Certainly we, as a nation of believers, can figure out a way to fund high-quality preschool-through-adult education. We talk about 'lifelong learners,' but why are the 'littlest learners' so neglected?

This investment will return in big ways. Today, some cities and states are focusing efforts on expanding existing daycare or adding daycare programs. So it has started. Keep watching for preschool to pop up in parent websites, as well as scholarly reports. There are so many implications and ramifications.

'Life Rules' start in preschool.

Preschool models basic 'life rules' children will always keep, such as sharing and caring, taking turns, saying "sorry," and cleaning up messes. Of course, academic skills are important, but so are recess, dramatic play, being kids. Getting dirty. Creating. Building. Singing and dancing.

Preschool doesn't have to be kindergarten or first grade, and shouldn't. However, every child deserves a chance to participate, gain basic social skills, learn and grow. How developmentally appropriate can preschools be in a digital era? Such a conversation!

I commend Head Start as a marvelous achievement, but not all kids are being served and I want to see every youngster in programs. Don't you? It's a matter of equity. Children who are not in decent daycare, or a solid preschool, are starting school already behind and just get further behind. Statistics are statistics, no point in stating the obvious.

Preschools model empathy, cooperation, and team building.

Preschools teach empathy and cooperation and build learning communities and teams. These skills are useful throughout school and into the world of work. There is no fluff about learning to work together. We simply don't know what jobs will be needed in the future, but communication and cooperation, 'soft skills' modeled in preschool, stay for life.

Since we live in a time of rapid paced innovation, it only makes sense to kick off quality programs right from the get-go, or again, kids are already behind before they even start. That certainly does not level the playing field.

Take care of preschool teachers: respect and pay fairly.

We need to rethink the importance of early-start learning and fully fund universal preschool.

I'd certainly like to see monies redirected from prisons to preschools, wouldn't you?

Let's also reflect on standards for becoming a preschool teacher and perceived status, compared to 'regular' school. What about low teacher pay, combined with big responsibilities. It's quite an important job. The academic push has pushed all the way down now, and pressure is on our preschool teachers and tiny tots.

I read that there were a few years during World War II that universal preschool was fully funded. When that brief stint ended in 1946, it was 'get the best you can get.' I know. I've been there, too; sadly, it was while I was a principal, taking care of everybody else's children.

Now that Peanut (my granddaughter, Morgan) is getting ready to start kindergarten at the 'big school' and leave her preschool, I find myself torn in two directions.

I love helping at a great preschool.

Ironic I love to hang with the small ones. I began my career by student teaching in seventh and eighth grade reading, followed by high school English, Speech, Drama, and Reading.

While Principal, I learned about preschool in real-time, on the job training. Since the preschool was on our K-6 campus, for a couple years I was given the entire preschool program, as well. Not knowing what I was doing, I was the worst, but well-intended. I just loved those kids!

Preschool is bliss, simply bliss. I've had such a great time at Morgan's preschool, kind of a combo of Reggio and Montessori styles. Yet, not every child in American goes to a quality preschool. That's a fact. I want every child to have the best experience our little Peanut had.

I think we're going to see a deluge of articles regarding the intense need for universal preschool. With both parents working, a ton of single mothers juggling a lot of balls, time is a scarce commodity.

Combine children's need for dramatic play, exposure to the written and spoken word, learning how to learn and get along with each other, preschool teachers are the unsung heroes and sheroes deserving our thanks and admiration.

Volunteer at a preschool.

So I decided there is something I can do, to help at least one school. I'm volunteering now at summer camp preschool. When the fall term starts, I'm at school half days, every day to help with a newly funded reading program. I think I'll need a nap mat.

Here's how day one went.

Including a hike to park, but no swimming yet.

1. My tennies got soaked in grass at playground. Special!
2. Narrowly escaped flying balls at recess.
3. Remembered Kleenex, wipes & Band Aids in my pockets.
4. Can't sneak raspberries out of a baggie. Little eyes everywhere.
5. Rolls in the lunch program just as good as I remembered, not gluten free.
6. Little milk cartons still hard to open & straws get bent.
7. Velcro; or better practice shoe tying. Easier to walk when shoes are on right feet.
8. Remembering my Dollar Store sticker roll. Genius, hurray!

I'll be writing about my preschool adventures, you can be sure of that. Watching routines work and not work, having the kid slime me from his snail, and getting all those big smiles and hugs, what can be better? Preschool is blissful. Let's make it a top priority. Universal preschool. Now!

Leaving footprints on your reading hearts, Rita

6B

LEARNING TO READ, COVERED WITH JELLO, BUGS AND SNAILS!

September 24, 2016

'Little People Learning Land,' a world of wonder. Week one.

It's one thing to read and write about literacy, it's another to breathe it. The last time I had a crazy notion in my head I ended up teaching with teachers in over five hundred K-12 classrooms.

At this stage, it's unfathomable I would dive headfirst into the murky waters of preschool. It's so rewarding but extremely demanding. Good thing I got my 'little' on.

I was blessed to join a staff of two teacher-directors. Their five-star preschool qualified for one of the coveted special new grants for early literacy; that's where I come in. Tonight I'm writing from head and heart, sharing highlights of my first week in 'Little People Learning Land.' I hope it inspires you, brings a smile, validates what you are doing, maybe a couple tears of joy tossed into the recipe.

Ready to teach, starting year forty-six.

1. Get organized. Favorite stories, puppets.
2. Psych myself I can do this!
3. Freak out, play calming music. Breathe.
4. Contemplate bowing out…for about thirty seconds.

5. Model positive lifelong learning and growth mindset.
6. Just do it. No layers of indecision. Walk the Talk.

Kids' learning goals and objectives:

1. Follow routines. Take turns.
2. Be kind, empathetic, share.
3. Practice communication skills.
4. Learn through play.
5. Have fun!!!

A portrait of our class.

The kids are diverse; so beautiful. It's an inclusive class, with children coming and going certain days of the week, staying half day or full day, or all week. The total class size on any day is sixteen, perfect, split with three teachers.

Some kids come from special programs. They thrive with blocks, Legos, play, large and small motor activities, singing rhymes, songs, and making rhythms. We are the school counselors, nurses, librarians, and most importantly: teachers. I am not taking any credit. The two teachers are an extraordinary wife-husband cohesive teaching pair who have been working together a long time.

They are simply perfect for the children. Me? Creating a tripod of assistance to two amazing people. That's all. Call me lucky to be there.

Description of the school and curriculum.

Use your imagination. The main floor of the house has an extensively supplied art room, stage area, interest areas (centers), writing stations, computers, separate room with kidney small-group table and every conceivable developmentally appropriate learning tool. Upstairs off limits to the children, books, and to-do activities, tutus, tap shoes, instruments, dramatic play activity kits, years of collecting.

Outside is the primary focus of school, its gardens, enormous variety of play structures, roller skates, sand and water play tables, bikes, discovery areas, toys and games, loads of ball hoops and balls. Obstacle courses, running, jogging, and exercising are interwoven into literacy concepts. Picnic tables, and little tables and chairs are used for snacks, meals and outdoor lessons.

A developmentally appropriate school, movement, arts, music, science, technology, and advanced basic skills curriculum predominate. Preschoolers show their creativity through ongoing projects, themes and teachable moments arising moment to moment. Going with the flow.

Before school started, we attended a two-day training session on implementing the early literacy grant. Now we're applying what we learned. Because we work in close proximity all day long, it offers collaborative opportunity to learn from each other. There are no prescriptive guidelines; already a pretty finely etched class program, just right for all the children. The assessment piece is currently in review.

Learning Team: Children and teachers.

The school is organized into learning pairs, one 'bigger' and one 'littler' per team. This is truly multi-age teaching at its finest. Empathy, kindness, rules to honor and live by. "Please" and "thank you." No exceptions allowed. Through a highly structured environment, the day goes smoothly with its inherent rituals, fluid curriculum, loads of play, and scientific discovery. Really messy. Really active. These two are the most creative teachers I have ever worked with. Family now.

Literacy all day, everywhere.

The other day we took a neighborhood walk. The kids had pails looking for objects such as acorns, etc. We were naming sounds and letters throughout the walk. Neighbors came out to say hello and conversations stimulated language development. Snails were the hit. Every kiddo wanted a snail. The previous day while we were gardening, worms ruled.

It's interesting to develop on-the-spot literacy lessons during a nature neighborhood walk—even better than a typical classroom gallery walk. Every day there is some sort of project; early versions of project-based learning are abundant.

Children read to each other, I read while they eat breakfast, snack, and during lunch, before nap, small and large group, one-to-one. 'Biggers' read to the 'littler' partners.

The best literacy research is extremely important. But tonight I am more concerned with how I invigorate my reading lessons into children's real-world interests: bugs, snails, with cause & effect, scientific investigation, discovery, art, music and movement...you get the idea.

More than ever I believe in dramatic play, environmental print, purposeful anchor charts, and language experience. Reading and writing always go together.

Creating a print- and language-rich environment.

1. Visual awareness of print.
2. Listening skills and phonemic awareness.
3. Context and meaning.
4. Reading and making books.
5. Making predictions.
6. Sequencing.
7. Speaking in complete sentences.
8. Building vocabulary orally and written.

I've been writing about the critical need for universal preschool. Lately I've noticed other articles, hopefully a trend of positive support for early literacy.

Budding readers and writers are joyous little learners. Pretty ironic, I've been teaching reading to students for so many years, and university-credential reading courses. Now these tiny kiddos.

Nothing prepared me for the sheer joy of wiping tears, handling minor disputes, cleaning Jello, getting shoes on the right feet, all the while teaching the foundations of literacy and love of reading. Impossible? No, not at all. Everything is possible. Just watch!

Leaving footprints on your reading hearts, Rita

6C

LEARNING TO TEACH LITTLEST ANGELS, LIFE LESSONS FOR ALL

November 29, 2016

Leaving a legacy. Walking the talk.

I never dreamed I'd take my biggest educational risk ever, teaching the 'littles,' but I did. Although for several years I was a preschool Principal, it's not the same as this.

After summer volunteering, a literacy grant was awarded to this special preschool, just my thing, so I'm back in the classroom again, helping out. I joined a wonderful multi-age, fully-included school, ages two-to-eight. That's quite a span to differentiate for. Right now, there are mostly 'littles,' ages two-to-five.

Tears, tantrums, need for Band Aids…and reassurance. They miss their mamas and daddies. Shoes on wrong feet, saying sorry, sharing and helping, spilling milk and dropping food, who knew? No just sitting around that kidney-shaped table.

Teaching every level of reading, university, high school English and Speech, was way easier, However, having the opportunity to watch Little Einsteins in action is astounding. Simply amazing!

We encourage ourselves and others to have a positive growth mindset, take risks, be bold, and model lifelong learning. But how many of us actually do it? It's easier to stay where we are, doing what is pretty familiar even with all the unknowns and constant change.

What I did was just drastic, but I almost feel like I know what I'm doing. It's truly like being a first year teacher and learning how to teach all over again.

I lucked out and learn from two extraordinary teacher-mentors, thirty- and fifteen-year veterans. I could only wish to teach this age group and needs one millionth as well. Simply a work of heart and art. Beautiful!

What makes this school great?

1. Consistent routines, rules, rewards, consequences. Manners key. Sharing. Happy!
2. Children served healthy meals and snacks four times a day, and attempt new foods.
3. Students each have a buddy all day long. 'Bigs' help 'littles,' with hand washing (constant), mats, reading, walking together, taking care of each other.
4. Children clean their own messes, tend gardens, share and trade toys, worms and bugs.
5. Helping each other with projects is the norm, project-based learning, 'littles-style.'
6. Literacy is highest focus, all day long. Visiting librarian, trips to library, reading, skills, three rotating groups throughout day. We're sneaky.
7. Lots of free and structured play, dramatic, manipulatives, stations, outdoor nature walks, and trips around neighborhood.
8. Focus on athletics and good health with exercises; breathing, recesses, and swim lessons.
9. Arts, music, science, technology, building and maker-spaces, 'Genius Hour' all day.
10. Emergent readers learning phonemic awareness, sounds, early writing, book handling, concepts of print.

It's a good thing I don't believe in failure, only feedback.

Starting over made me more humble. I always knew I was supposed to be teaching and I still know it, here. This experience has enriched my life. I pray I am leaving a positive legacy in my life.

Working with two extraordinary teachers, teaching way outside my comfort and capability zone, has made me a stronger, more interesting person I think. It's like gaining a new perspective.

Experiencing the world of 'Butch' the squirrel coming to the door for morning peanuts, digging for worms and finding snails as a bonus, sharing bikes and balls...this is the world we all need to be living in. Pure innocence, natural learning. Childhood is a precious thing, what's the rush, anyway?

Crying our tears after things don't go our way, words of encouragement from a 'little' to a 'little,' this is genuine empathy which cannot be taught, but modeled, oh yes. It does seem to come instinctively at this stage of life.

Speaking of development, our directors established a caring community of positive learners at this tender age, who are protective of their school, know the 'Pledge of Allegiance' and like to learn about endangered species, birds...you get the idea.

Assessing our young children.

This year the assessments flowed. And flowed and flowed. To my dismay I found myself categorizing and labeling many already labeled kiddos, and was supposed to give numerical scores to tasks way beyond preschool. Like *Leo the Late Bloomer,* sometimes the children are very grown-up and world-smart, other times, not so much. They need the gift of time. What's the rush, anyway?

Observing and measuring young children has trickled down, and is just crazy to me. But I did it, complaining and whining all the way. To my surprise I actually got some formative information I figured would be baseline data. I had to wrap my head around that. I was pretty surprised I had done a decent job in a number of cognitive areas already, but needed to improve my basic understanding of most basic student needs for this age. No expert anymore. Lifelong learner, that's me.

Adapting to the needs of youngest learners.

While I'm busy teaching how to use scissors, cut and paste, glue, stick cotton balls on Santa's beard, I'm reading books about snow, and probably playing *Little Mermaid* quietly.

I sing, stretch, hang out on the floor, build Legos and in between carry around my set of alphabet cards or a classic book, especially those with rhyme, rhythm and predictable patterns. Their favorite books so far are *Yo! Yes?*; *Chicka Boom Boom*; *Brown Bear, What Did You See?* They enjoy fiction and non-fiction. The most loved, well worn, non-fiction books are about China, sharks, and endangered species.

We've done a lot of book repair and scotch tape flows freely. It's a BIG deal. Before naps, I read with clusters of kids, and never have enough time to read their stacks. Sometimes I tell them to just pick a special page and that works for the moment. It also teaches skimming and scanning.

Bests. Stand-outs.

Favorite whole class Circle Lessons: *Tikki Tikki Tembo*, with rhythm instruments, *Everybody Cooks Rice*, using chopsticks, and *Ballet Shoes*. I brought my tap shoes. Best science experiment was 'Sinking Submarine,' that little old plastic sub cereal toy, powered by baking soda. We began learning the scientific method.

In rotating groups each day, I started with shapes, colors, numbers, counting. We used an old fashioned, large rotating hands teaching clock, wood teaching shoe, abacus, slates, and white boards. Lots of Play Dough. Dud lesson was tracing our names in salt trays. Salt flew all over the art room! Not doing that again. Teachers Cheryl and Tom are very patient with me, the children too.

Teaching emerging, budding readers to read.

Literacy skills so far are looking pretty strong. Concepts of print, phonemic awareness, rhyme and rhythm, a few sight words, alphabet, writing some letters and our names. Learning that sounds make letters and letters make words.

Reading, writing, speaking, and listening integrate with arts and crafts, nature projects, music and movement.

In addition to word recognition, I've been modeling comprehension by checking 'schema' (prior knowledge), making predictions, doing Book Walks, retellings and summarizing. A lot of sequencing. Basic story grammar. Pretty great for preschool kids, don't you agree? I ask questions on many levels of 'Bloom's Taxonomy,' which I never thought I could.

Young readers are amazing new word learners. I am constantly surprised at the words the kids are using; their vocabularies are increasing steadily. I haven't done a Word Wall in the art room, so that's maybe on my to-do list. I am, however starting pop-up cards and making books.

Most important, I think, we are modeling how to make our needs known, use complete sentences, discover the beauty of our language and the joy of reading. It just doesn't get any better than that.

Preschool is my ultimate joy.

I encourage us all to be bold, be brave, and take risks. That never changes. Exploring the passion bringing us, and keeping us teaching, cleaves us together, learners all.

Come experience preschool with me and you'll know what I mean. There's simply nothing better than love. I love you all. Let our voices 'raise the roof' with celebration of young scholars in waiting!

Leaving footprints on your reading hearts, Rita

6D

Did You Bring Seaweed Salad Today, Rita?

January 29, 2017

Happy New Year! Did you bring seaweed salad today, Rita?

Little kids are a riot. Big kids, too. All the same, really, just size variations. Some of the funniest things happen at school, pretty much all day long.

As the year rapidly draws to close and I'm sneaking in a few unexpected days off, I am also gearing up big time for what lands on Jan 2nd. I just checked out our school syllabus for winter/spring and I need about three of me to tackle even number one on the list.

Starting over in preschool was the best decision I ever made. I am finally learning how to teach. I think I have the basics down for this age group and took a lot of classes, which helped. My master teachers are extremely experienced and have my back, and sometimes my front. Talk about lifelong learning.

I just got moved back out of the art room, which I requested. Toys are in there, too and the distractions are the pits. Also, teachers Cheryl and Tom discovered I am really bad at crafts and they redid or finished whatever I had started.

So I am back where I really like it, the little room in the middle, with a kidney shaped table, alphabet on the walls, flannel and magnet boards, a chalkboard, and some storage. This is where I teach best. Our inner sanctum.

And just in time. Today I read expectations for the literacy grant I need to accomplish like the speed of light. (Multi-age, two-to-eight, fully included kiddos). Fortunately I like a challenge and believe me, I'm up to this. At least I hope so!

Expectations. What I have to do, ready or not.

- Basic skills, as expected, thematic.
- Teach about all fifty states.
- Teach where students live, grandma, etc.
- Teach fifty states in alphabetical order.
- Two spring concerts.

How I will accomplish my expectations.

- Never sit in teacher chair. Sit at eye-level on tiny, uncomfortable chairs.
- Always carry Kleenex in pockets, but check pockets before washer.
- Carry food in pockets. Kids are like magnets to you
- Wash hands all day. Keep lotion handy.
- Watch with eyes on all sides of head.
- Keep laser-like focus every minute.
- Kids are gross and like bugs, snails, and magnifying glasses.
- Wipe down playground equipment before their pants get wet.
- Expect spills. Pour minute amounts of milk, then refill.
- Model manners. "Please" and "thank you."
- One rule: Keep hands and feet to yourself.
- Each one, teach one, big with lil' buddy all day long.

Morning Circle. Love, love, love it!

I lead Circle Time two days a week: Mondays and Wednesdays. I like to start off with a strong 'Set,' or opener, based on a theme, featuring a favorite classic book.

I have fun bringing in old things like my tap shoes. Since the children are taught tap by Teacher Cheryl, they have prior knowledge. The kids all got to try on my mother's beaded shoes she had made in Hong Kong, which leads to another lesson.

That's my best teaching: those 'Aha!' teachable moments. Children's questions and direct experiences focus and shape the lesson. I just provide something to work with once the kids' natural interest starts my creative side glowing.

Hands on, minds-on reading for youngest learners.

Sometimes I bring in a little talking plastic box, chatter teeth, or gag…then I always tie in with the story for the day. Sneaking in 'Story Grammar,' or elements, happens a lot. Making reading manipulatives works great. So far we've made a pop up flash card, four and eight box-folds, etc. I plan to start making more books.

Book handling has been a huge focus. I've been modeling concepts of print, left and right. Of most fun, kids have used tons of scotch tape, repairing books. I never thought I'd need to model how to gently turn book pages, but I notice all the children being careful with their chosen books and wanting a lot of tape to repair miniscule tears they find in older, loved books. We are creating a culture of loving books.

We are already making predictions, sequencing, and summarizing. Phonemic awareness (sounds), singing constantly. (I sing badly and never remember all the words.) Some nursery rhymes. Doing things I thought were impossible only a few months ago. Some of the kids are starting to get 'word families,' so I'm using books with rhyme, rhythm, and predictable patterns. A lot of *Brown Bear, Brown Bear, What Do You See? and Chicka Chicka Boom Boom!*

Monday is 'Show and Tell,' my highlight of the week.

Our Directors modeled a winning strategy for 'Show and Tell.' Not only is it meaningful for the moment, our teachers start getting children ready for upcoming programs by experiencing quick performances with their peers. We are their audience.

It's really special. Of course, the kiddos bring their weird, special toy or other object, maybe a leaf, never know. They take their turn and add birthday, age, and respond to questions posed by the teachers. I laugh a lot and feel happy.

Literacy is all day, every day, varied kinds of literacy.

Here's just a little bit of the fun.
- Stations and Maker Spaces. Technology.
- Teaching toys, for large and small motor.
- Arts, music, dance, swimming classes. Fabulous teachers. (No, not me).
- Library visiting, and at-school visits by a fabulous storyteller.
- Reading during breakfast, snacks as appropriate, and not distracting.
- 'Reading the room' all day. Charts, functional (real life) print.
- Reading groups. I assist teachers with three small groups a day. Mini-lessons.
- Reading on mats before nap. Alone, to each other, or by teachers.
- I like to put books with bookmarks in their cubbies, sometimes a sticker.

Circle Time. A really funny story.

"Did you bring seaweed salad, today, Rita?"

I read the book *Everybody Cooks Rice* and brought chopsticks. We used them to sort, count, and pick up raisins (which of course, got eaten). That day for lunch I brought Japanese food for lunch, including seaweed salad. The two-year-old kept asking about it. It was green and looked gross, probably smelled gross too, but intriguing. I knew he, and a bunch of other kids, wanted to taste it.

Every day after that for several weeks, the children would ask when I came into school "What's in your pockets today? Maybe a beanbag, floating eyeball, who knows? Then always, "Did you bring seaweed salad, today, Rita?"

So, right before Christmas vacation I bought a large carton of seaweed salad. The teachers knew the joke, so asked me to put the seaweed salad on the children's plates, first. A few kids tried it and said "eww," etc. A couple who did, just loved it and ate a bunch. Lunch was quickly served when one 'little' thought seaweed salad was all he was going to get and started crying. Greatly relieved when, a second later, lunch was served.

Art Linkletter had a great show for many years when I was a 'little,' myself. One of his weekly segments was called "Kids Say the Darndest Things." True! I never know what the 'littles' are going to say or do, so it keeps me on my toes.

It's another rainy day in Eugene, the horrid ice storm is over, we weathered the storm, and read a lot of books. On the worst ice days, except one, I still made it to school. I managed to get to the Dollar Store for school art supplies.

After all, a day without the 'littles' isn't as special. The most lovely thing in a long time was the Christmas concert, but that too, is over now. Spring Concert to look forward to, and prepare for, no small feat.

Children of all ages warm us to see the new and good in all things, to feel our hearts beating.

It's my pleasure to be among the first to say a most Happy New Year to you and yours. To fresh starts and new beginnings. Let us share New Year's hopes, dreams, and wishes for the literacy lives and good life of all our children.

This time of year, as we reflect hope and dream our dreams, I wish a blessed, healthy, Happy New Year to you, your school and home families. Take time to share the children's stories and laugh with colleagues and loved ones.

Leaving footprints on your reading hearts, Rita

6E

LET'S START AT THE VERY BEGINNING!
March 5, 2017

"Let's start at the very beginning. It's a very good place to start. When we read we begin with A, B, C...." Who knew I'd love teaching 'littles?' Not me, that's for sure.

Month-seven teaching preschool, update.

Here's my learning update, month-seven of my, "What was I thinking in year forty-six???" Who else in their right mind would start over, at the very beginning? Like how to hold a pencil, how to handle a book with love and how to repair ripped pages? I think I'm doing pretty well with the goals of the literacy grant, but I'm not working in sequential order like I usually do. I feel so out of sync, when all of a sudden, "Voila!" The pieces come together.

Show and Tell and Circle Time offer time to structure the day, hold a class meeting for a couple minutes, sing, stretch and say our positive affirmations. I help our teachers by leading Circle Time two days a week, a learning celebration to whet their appetites for more, with puppets, props, a costume, stories, you know where I'm going here. Comfy family learning.

Miracles occur routinely now. The little girl who only just called me 'mama' and wouldn't speak, now calls me 'Rita,' and participates in most activities, knows shapes, colors, uses complete sentences, and glows! She's pretty close on right and left shoes, too. Her mom comes at half day and I always make sure to tell her what a great day this little learner had and show her various math, writing and US states work projects. I am amazed and humbled.

Spending days with young children is joyful and frequently a riot. I never know what's going to happen next. Now a big believer in Velcro and easy zip jackets—not hoodies. One's perspective on teaching changes dramatically. I bought a warm, puffy coat with detachable hood, extra gloves with a bit of grip, trike-proof shoes; so all set for action, and there's always something.

Teaching Researcher in the world of young children.

As a 'teaching researcher,' my leap to budding readers was a big stretch, and to be honest, really challenging for me. Much of the time I am no super star, the Directors are though, and I am fortunate they help me much (or most) of the day.

Our school is now floating with 'littles,' ages two-to-six. There are only a few older kids to be role models, and that's necessary, the way our Directors set up the program. Children have buddies all day long.

We got a new kid a couple days ago. The day the family came to check out the school, I nearly flipped. It takes a lot to make me nervous, but I was. The little guy was flying through the school and at recess, was a major pain. I need to figure out how to reach and teach him. So far I have an 'F.'

For a number of years I presented for Head Start, Early Childhood Education, and Kindergarten Conferences, but this was not the same as planning transformative strategies, while simultaneously meeting youngsters' most basic needs.

A couple times I've asked kids what they ate for dinner and I hear "cereal." Makes one think and be grateful we can feed the children at school. In addition, meals offer opportunity to model the proper way to hold utensils, cut, pour, clean up messes, and have good manners.

No one leaves their tables until dismissed. Routines don't vary and 'littles' obviously crave the structure.

What I learned this week.

1. Must better differentiate instruction for Circle Time and small group. I have three smaller groups each day, with children extremely varied in skill needs.
2. The kids are so smart! When I plan closely knit lessons with room to toss out as I go, I have some 'Aha!' moments and know I am teaching at pretty advanced levels conceptually, high challenge, low threat.
3. DAP, 'developmentally appropriate practices' is absolutely the way to go. Learning through play at the various stations, in and outdoors, makes perfect sense.
4. To keep faith. There are several children I thought I could not reach, and they are blossoming with language.
5. Our administrators are miracle workers. This time I am the follower. They are the leaders and what I see them do with children even I had no hope for, is truly a gift.
6. Kids are engaged by making Teacher Cheryl's pizzas, looking at worms through their magnifiers, playing with magnets, reading all day long. Their little hands like to be active, touching everything, especially my lunch. They also smell, taste and learn through all modalities. Teaching 'lefties' to read and write is interesting to me.
7. Teaching hygiene is really important. Our kids also got dental kits and are expected to do thorough hand washing, while reciting the ABC's. In fact, I've probably spent more time on hand washing than teaching reading this year, well maybe not, it just seems like it.
8. By unleashing my creativity and taking risks, my teaching is better. I wish I was a better artist, but I'm having fun and attempting more than in the beginning of the year.

9. I am still not great at structuring transitions for this age. The packed daily schedule is etched into my head because there is so much to do and never enough time. I am always late, though, and generally the teachers come to get me. Once in flow, I hate to stop.

10. Patience and humility are what I learned most this week. I've got a lot to learn.

It seems so obvious to me that all kids should have the opportunity to attend preschool. What we do, matters.

Learning is especially significant for these youngsters who come from circumstances less than ideal, needing every bit of my already tired brain and body at top notch to level the playing field, at least for these kids. I know what I know now about teaching in a multi-age-inclusive school for youngest learners. I know what I don't know, and hope to learn: sign language, needlework, (maybe) coding, hope so, and better use of technology for this age.

I've pretty well mastered how to model sharing and caring, resolving disputes with other ways than hitting. As for the literacy grant, even the three-year-olds are picking up more advanced concepts such as word families (*at, cat, sat, mat*, etc.). I love multi-age instruction because the children teach each other.

Here are some basic skills I've been teaching:

- Tracing, cutting, holding a regular pencil
- Book handling
- Concepts of print
- Rhyme, rhythm and predictable patterns
- Alphabet, (upper and lower case)
- Phonemic awareness (sounds, word play)
- Basic Phonics (Sounds and letters,)
- Writing name and basic sight words
- Writing and counting numbers 1-20
- Punctuation basics

- Sequencing, order of things
- Comprehension, Book Walks, Story parts

I believe in Universal Preschool with all my heart. America's youngest learners deserve a joyous pre-kinder experience, not just daycare. We are family. We offer children a home for the mind and heart and a sanctuary for the soul.

Teaching preschool meant starting over, after a lengthy career at all levels. Taking early childhood education courses, first aid and constant mentoring and modeling by our teachers helped me. I started at the very beginning, like a first year teacher, not a teacher of teachers.

I think I am moderately successful, a least some of the time. I am not sure what that really looks like for me. But even if I am not at my finest, I hope the children know I am giving them my all, love, that is, and in the end of things, isn't that what really matters?

Leaving footprints on your reading hearts, Rita

6F

TEACHING LITTLEST KIDS TO READ...OR NOT?
September 23, 2017

'Littles' say the funniest things!

The other day I asked "What's your mommy's name?" Reply: Mommy." Get what you ask for, right?

Childhood is a precious time. What's the rush?

Childhood is a precious time. What's the rush?

I'm back at school, year two, one week in, hired under a Literacy Grant, a good thing: and not so good. What's great is I have an opportunity to fine-tune teaching littlest learners, emergent readers. I was really winging it last year.

Students who returned are lots bigger, now the 'biggers,' having moved up the ladder.

They still ask what's in my lunch, check out my pockets for little surprises, and give me so many slimy hugs I already have my first cold. 'Littles' are germy, but so darn cute.

Not so great: academic expectations put on these tiny children. It's one thing to level the playing field by giving kids a head start on their learning.

Oh, can't neglect to mention feeding kiddos breakfast, lunch, and two healthy snacks a day (food in their tummies they might not get at home).

However, on my third day back, our Directors handed me the first stack of assessments for the kids. The three of us have batches to complete. We are of course, watching and listening; anecdotal observation still the best way to see where kids are, in my opinion. The rest, a waste of time at this age, maybe every stage. We are in agreement.

A big believer in formative assessment for 'littles,' we look at motor skills, affective domain, basic Maslow needs, and Dewey interests. Some children do not know how to hold a pencil, much less write with one.

We know children learn through play, cooking, arts, crafts, gardening, and extensive outdoor education. Sensory tables, maker spaces, centers, library visits, and field trips. No different than older kiddos, really.

Our children clean their messes, say "please" and "thank you," are polite, generally well behaved and so loving in our school family. They are indeed rays of sunshine and fill our buckets with joy each day.

The students also do community service, performing at several nursing homes. Developmentally appropriate activities are highlights all day long. As it should be.

The school Director-Teachers features Show and Tell, amazing Circle Times each morning, creates meaningful child-centered, self-selected activities throughout the day, as well as small group instruction, mini-lessons on basic skills that make sense.

Basic skills for 'littles?'

Now my concern. What should basic skills be and look like for youngest learners? How serious should we be about teaching reading for littlest kiddos, when I already feel it's way too academic in kindergarten—and now down to preschool? Good question for us all to ponder.

Our school serves kids coming to us from several programs, making this diverse, inclusive school a wondrous place to be. Older kiddos graduated to kindergarten in May, so this year we serve the littlest 'litttles,' ages two-to-five, with a lot of three and four year olds.

I've been teaching reading at one level or another, including University credential reading courses, for forty -six years, including during my Principalship, Pre-6. I am pretty sure I know what we should be teaching and how to create meaningful learning experiences for emergent readers. But I question myself now, I admit.

Yesterday our kids were fixated on a spider walking on the ceiling, a ladybug and worm at recess, and how to build a tower with blocks and Legos. They also love books; reading is a big part of our day, but not necessarily the skills-driven curriculum we need to 'cover.' Is it really ok to teach a sequential skill set when the kids are already all over the place in schoolhouse requirements?

I started working nearly immediately on the literacy grant curriculum standards, very advanced for our children. Then I happened to read an affirming article on Facebook from Huffington Post, by Gaye Groover Christmus, "4 Things Worse than Not Learning to Read in Kindergarten." Much earlier I had blogged for BAM Radio Network, "Dick and Jane Go to Kindergarten. Yikes!" My feeling are apparent.

So this is not my first rodeo commentary about what youngest learners should know and do in reading.

I am clueless why in the U.S. we are forced 'to the Core,' putting terrible pressure on teachers and kids. We are aware some children do not get reading until later, maybe seven or eight, then it all clicks in. Some children are ready, many are not. I'd better not hear about another boy being held back in kindergarten for his immaturity (nearly always boys) and being a non-reader. Think *Leo the Late Bloomer.*

All the little flowers in our 'garden of reading' bloom differently, at different times.

Retaining children who are not reading at the end of Kindergarten makes one question the wisdom, or lack of, in pressuring teachers, parents, and children, when reading is a natural evolution, not revolution. Children all learn best their own way, at their own pace, so it's pretty ridiculous to say all kids will read by such and so date.

If we really want to encourage joyful, lifelong readers we really need to take a look at expectations and invite policymakers to teach with us; spend a day, maybe two, to get a better understanding of what's going on with kiddos today, and what we need to teach. Get a grip, people! We're pushing young children beyond what's developmentally appropriate. And that can backfire, creating dislike, or even hate, of reading.

I decided a long time ago that doing Keynotes and training was great, but it was far better to 'Walk the Talk,' then 'Talk the Walk'... so back into classrooms I went, leading me all the way back from high school English to preschool. What an adventure!

Here's where I start with emergent readers:

1. Book Handling: What a book is, looking at front and back covers, pictures, photos, how to gently turn pages. Left and right, a big deal at this age. Print goes from left-to-right in English.
2. I look for lefties: It may make a difference how I teach tracking (following the lines of print).
3. Concepts of print: Print awareness. Thought can be written. Print is interesting, sounds make letters, letters make words. There are spaces between words. Words make sentences.
4. Phonemic awareness is fun to teach. We play with speech sounds, manipulate letters to make words.
5. Rhyming is perfect at this age, think *Brown Bear, Jesse Bear*, etc.

6. We sing, chant, move, play instruments, clap beats. Reading is rhythmic. Alphabet! *Chicka Chicka ABC.*

7. Our print and language-rich environment includes dramatic play, environmental and functional print: the three biggies.

8. Our books feature rhyme, rhythm, and predictable patterns. Picture books are wonderful for young readers, as well.

9. We read in increments all day. Lap reading, small group storytelling, reading nook before rest time, sharing books with each other.

Reading is a celebration! Books tell stories about new friends and places, interesting animals—like sharks—plus interesting people.

I also use language experience, encourage vocabulary, teach beginning comprehension through making predictions, retellings, summarizing, basic story grammar and sequence, as in *Give a Mouse a Cookie.* I think that's all darn good, appropriate stuff.

We write, using inventive spelling. Through play activities, our kiddos learn to first identify sounds, next write corresponding letters, sound-symbol correspondence. They are not ready for cueing. I work on writing their name as soon as they recognize the alphabet has meaning, not just singing it. Names are important to start with. I read the book *Chrysanthemum.*

I also love teaching the book *Yo! Yes?* Not only is it perfect for encouraging friendships, sharing and caring; basic punctuation is easy and fun to teach with this story.

My point is that I believe our school is teaching at a very high level, with high expectations in a variety of necessary emergent reading behaviors, and corresponding low threat.

Using reading manipulatives such as magnet letters on cookie sheets is a super way for us to learn our language, hands-on. Painting, drawing, clay, dough, puppets, fun!

So I know I lucked out learning from our outstanding Directors, and I understand there are strings with any grant money, of course. But

I believe it's also important to take a step back and see what outcomes are supposed to look like, what standards need to be met.

So, seriously, let's look at our grant standards in one area, jumping right in for emergent readers with "Phonological Awareness and Emergent Reading." They are simply not ready at two-four years old, several with 'special' needs, Spanish speaking, to master these skills. Check out this list from our grant assessments, due shortly:

1. Demonstrates phonological awareness skills.
   1.1. Uses rhyming skills.
   1.2. Segments sentences and words.
   1.3. Blends single letters and syllables.
   1.4. Identifies same and different sounds at the beginning and end of words.

2. Uses letter-sound associations to sound out and write words.
   2.1. Writes words using letter sounds.
   2.2. Sounds out words.
   2.3. Produces correct sounds for letters.

3. Reads words by sight.
   3.1. Identifies letter names.

Etc. Phew!

You tell me: Is this where we want to go as a nation of readers teaching and encouraging young learners and readers? Skills-driven, outcome-based preschool readers? I think not.

Modeling the love and joy of reading fairy tales, classic stories, adventures, fiction and non-fiction, oh that's what it's all about, isn't it?

Leaving footprints on your reading hearts, Rita

6G

LIFE LESSONS FROM 'LITTLES!'

October 20, 2017

How do you spell love?

Literacy on little angel wings. Such joy, the most amazing learning experience of my life.

Learning to teach preschool.

Here's my update, year-two preschool, teaching kiddos emergent skills of reading and writing. Well, a lot more than that. Never sure who's teaching whom. 'A day in the passionate life,' so to speak. Since I wrote about the infamous pre-kinder assessments, I'm into the sheer joy of teaching and learning from the kids, who are my best teachers. There are so many life lessons, sometimes minute to minute.

I walk into school, immediately surrounded by sticky fingers, hugs, and checking out whether I have on my Minnie Mouse rainbow light-up watch. Loaded down with bags of mini-lessons, supplies, my lunch bag, and layers, I barely make it to our little middle room to organize in about three minutes. I feel like the Pied Piper. "Good morning, Teacher Rita!"

I already told you I am really bad with crafts, so back out of the art room, the big room so distracting; at home in the middle room, with all my favorite things: calendar, maps and globe, alphabet, flannel boards, our little table and chairs, and loads of teaching sets, readers and books. In the corner is a huge beanbag with big stuffies and pillow. We read there a lot. And talk. And I listen.

My room has a big teacher chair, but I prefer to sit in the little chairs, and I'm small anyway…or I lay on the floor with the kids. I like to be right at their eye level so I don't miss a single expression or nuance. I never know what life lessons will pop out.

Kids really do say the darndest things and observing their interactions is simply stunning.

"What's 'learning,' Teacher Rita? I know…it's letters and stuff!" Our youngest learners, ages two-through-five, teach us a great deal about life, its natural wonders, excitement of mastering what seems so simple, yet profound. Like how to hold a pencil, cut with scissors. You know, that kind of stuff.

New tablets arrived. The University of Oregon donated them and is involving our tiny children in a special program technology-based reading program. I'm going to learn so much!

I work in the best of all worlds, play, sign language, dance, swimming, arts, and gymnastics. Of course, basic math, reading, grammar, and everything you can imagine and probably more. For kids with labels or not, it is a multi-age, fully-included heaven. The Teacher Directors are extraordinary, program exemplary. I have nothing to do with that; I am a learner, learning how to teach and reach these children every day.

First, second, and third chances matter, even at this tender age. Just like *Leo The Late Bloomer*, our children are blooming at their own rate. And it's spectacular.

I'm sure we all agree that our life has to mean something; we need to have a passion and purpose. I'm wondering now if I was meant to do this, and what encouraged me in this millennium, to follow a hunch, take the biggest risk ever and savor the sweetness of teaching tiny kiddos.

It all has to start somewhere.

Why not me? I can do this. I am, and each day the children lead the way, life-lessons in bold neon, when I am receptive and not distracted. I give my all, with laser-like focus, eyes and ears seeing, feeling, and knowing what is being offered to me.

On my most exhausting days when I again ponder my sanity of this chosen course, the proverbial epiphany drops into my head and I heave a sigh of relief and laugh.

Each day I watch, listen, and participate in an extraordinary learning experience for me—probably way more than the children are getting. I am really learning how to teach. The art and craft of teaching, at its most basic Maslow (needs), Dewey (interests) and yes, 'Bloom's Taxonomy' (questioning).

What I've figured out on my own.

1. Model teamwork with my mentors and the children. What they see is what they do.
2. Be over-prepared. Plan for variations in variations, three small groups a day, plus teachable moments. 'Circle Time' is a big opener.
3. Model soft skills during outdoor education and recesses throughout day. Pilates. Brain Gym.
4. Daily calendar, about three minutes worth, teach in 10-15 min. chunks including story, skill, and hands-on activity (no worksheets). Levels within levels. Differentiating within differentiating.
5. Include multi-sensory strategies and DAP-worthy (developmentally appropriate practice) lesson design. Make mid-course corrections. Keep routine, but enliven my lessons. Students self-select seating, learning activities, help each other...and me.

6. Old fashioned, time-tested staples: Globe, maps, abacus, teaching clock, magnet boards and letters, flannel boards. Books. Reading and writing, Dramatic play centers, maker spaces, Legos.

7. Do what I do well; everything literacy. The rest? I learn as I go.

What I think is super important for little learners.

1. Be a friend and mentor.
2. Every 'little' age two and three has a bigger mentor who helps all day long: meal preparation, clean up, getting mats out, putting shoes on right feet, and getting that jacket on. 'Reading' to each other. Hugs and words. Console one another.
3. Clean up your mess. Everybody helps clean school. Everybody! Be kind and considerate. Take turns.
4. Teach each other. Share what you know.
5. Treat worms, bugs—all nature—with respect and care. No squishing!
6. "Please" and "thank you" go a long way.

Life Lessons from kids to us.

1. May the joy and wonder of learning continue from Pre-K through adult. We learn together. Lifelong learning: Lesson number one.
2. Kiddos clamor to play with my red 'Minnie Mouse' watch that lights up. They take turns pushing the tiny button that makes the colors revolve. Learning to wait and take turns: Life lesson number two.
3. The children model empathy, they just don't know the name. That's surely Life Lesson number three.
4. Curiosity is natural. Nurturing it and discovering genius in every child: Life Lesson number four.

5. Each child is part of the larger learning community, a caring place with buckets of sunshine. Life Lesson number five has to be making relationships, children to teachers, children to each other, teacher to teacher, and teacher to parents.

By modeling a caring, lifelong learning community comprised of our school, neighbors, nursing homes, swimming pool, library (you get the idea), our children have opportunity to prove they are super star learners.

In closing, one little guy left for kindergarten, 'the big school.' He comes back for day care after school. His mama picked him up tonight and made this heartwarming observation: "He is doing great in kindergarten. He is so ready. He is way ahead in all his academic skills, and because of this little school, he is excelling and happy."

Legacy, one minute, one hour, one day at a time.

Leaving footprints on your reading hearts, Rita

CHAPTER 7

DREAM THE DREAM,
LIVING A LIFE OF PURPOSE
Teacher Modeling Empathy: Living a Life of Purpose.

Chapter seven, small but mighty, highlights my life as a servant leader—as well as follower. I have always known my purpose was to teach. I believe that along the way I have reached a lot of kids and adults. I know I keep learning and growing. Maintaining my humility has been easy these last years, as I have been sorely tested. In this moment, *Lessons from Geese* stands out because I hear geese honking overhead! As our world grows ever-closer, I pray we learn from each other and celebrate goodness, diversity and beauty. Several of my stories share commonalities, stunning views of everyday life, and strengthen our resolve as citizens of the world.

A) Market Street, Bus Ride into Empathy
B) State of the Dream in the New Year
C) Finding Love Again
D) *Everybody Cooks Rice*
E) *Lessons from Geese*, Revisited: Leadership and Life

7A

MARKET STREET, BUS RIDE INTO EMPATHY
April 28, 2018

Empathy.

Empathy. Can't teach it; surely can model it. *Last Stop on Market Street,* 2015, a Newberry Medal, Caldecott Honor Book, and winner of other prestigious awards, reads as a modern masterpiece for children of all ages.

Not only does it appear to be a gentle, intergenerational love story between a boy and his grandma, we experience diversity, kindness, and empathy throughout this simple story.

This book radiates joy and the most lovely descriptions of a beautiful world. A world, maybe not so readily apparent until we really look beyond the obvious. Which is what we all certainly need to do.

Let's take a bus ride together, on Market Street.

Let's take a bus ride, a very special one. Just us, like Nana and CJ, the main characters in this heartwarming urban tale.

Yesterday I went on the bus with my granddaughter, Morgan, for her first grade field trip. She was so excited! I did a sleepover the night before. She woke me up about two hours before time for school, all dressed with lunch sack ready.

Going on the bus for her was a one-time event, for other children in this world it is routine, mundane—or maybe not, depending who Grandma is.

Before bed we shared *Last Stop on Market Street*. Had to get ready for our bus ride. Singing 'Wheels on The Bus' was good enough before, but at seven, maybe opening our eyes to the possibility that bus ride would be a good thing. And it was. Watching the world swirl by the bus, instead of staring at a Kindle.

Life lesson number one: Really live it.

I wasn't sure if a seven-year-old could comprehend the complexities of this story. Wrong. Morgan totally blew me away with her responses to what the main characters thought, felt, and did.

It turns out she had some 'schema,' or background knowledge about seeing the world through a different lens. Her mama had taken her to visit a family friend she helped out, who lived pretty close to where people came for food, clothes, and shelter from cold. Real life. Empathy for those in tough times, short or longer.

Morgan also knows about people who have no places to live. How can we shelter our children from the misfortunes of others when we see homeless people in tents or on street corners? Empathy for those less fortunate.

About the book.

Look at the cool front and back covers of this book. Can you make a prediction what the story is about? Do you know the author and artist? Such beautiful pictures!

Last Stop on Market Street offers us a magical time to look at what's really important in life; an opportunity to do a little soul searching and values clarification.

This story is perfect for everyone. For kiddos who may have too much, it's a real eye opener. For all of us, looking at the world with

Grandma offers a rare chance to truly see the myriad characters, not only on the bus or the neighborhood, but in life.

Where is the bus going?

The story begins with Nana and CJ leaving church to take a bus… to where? We don't know. All we know is that CJ is tired of the Sunday routine, longs for a car like his friend Colby. Wants what he doesn't think he has.

Early in the story we meet Mr. Dennis, a rich, colorful character, who happens to be the bus driver. He is quite entertaining and does little magic tricks for CJ and other passengers. More unique people are on that bus, and come on the bus at each stop. One by one, Nana makes sure to greet everyone and models that for CJ, who follows suit.

What a bus ride! A guy plays the guitar, we meet a lady with butterflies in a jar. People are chatting about everyday friends and interesting places. There is a hum of friendship and love in that bus.

Being with CJ's Nana, we share the world through her eyes, such a beautiful figurative, lyrical language. That's worth a choral response, chanting some of the lines together, such as: "He saw sunset colors swirling over crashing waves. Saw a family of hawks slicing through the sky. Saw the old woman's butterflies dancing free in the light of the moon."

Feel empathy for life through 'mind pictures,' first Nana, then CJ. It takes a little time for CJ to open his eyes and heart though. At first he is stuck by what he doesn't have and wants, before he understands Nana's worldview.

CJ asks Grandma why he can't 'just do nothing' after church like his friends. "I feel sorry for those boys," she told him. "They'll never get a chance to meet Bobo or the Sunglass Man." Perspective, right?

Then the blind man boards the bus. CJ learns he can, however, see the world in other ways, which helps CJ start to tune into the world he is missing.

CJ is learning there is a beautiful world around him, not about having a car, an iPad, or 'doing nothing,' but living the best life through meeting new interesting people, enjoying the clear air, and dancing butterflies. And CJ starts hearing the songs in his head played by the man with the guitar; the new rhythms are easily replicated, using all his senses.

An amazing world, because of a bus ride into empathy for himself and others. We still don't know what the final bus ride into empathy really entails, but each step along the way tantalizes and evokes a small (or maybe not so small) response in our heart and soul.

As we experience CJ's life lessons from Nana and the characters met along the way, each bus stop reminds me of each point in life, where we may hesitate, take a breath, then open ourselves to what's new, interesting, and of greater value than anticipated, or even noticed before.

Finally comes the bus driver's call, "Last stop on Market Street." What in the world can that stop be? I had no idea when I made my prediction, but Morgan did, right away. She even figured out the ending. I'm not giving that away...I know you'll want to read and share this book.

A life of purpose.

Anyway, off the bus, in a not-so-great, pretty dirty and raggedy urban neighborhood, CJ acts upset again. Nana makes everything better. Nana knows how to do it. And then....CJ sees familiar faces popping out of the windows. Old friends counting on him to show up and be the good person he is, every Sunday.

CJ feels warm and excited. He knows why he is there. His sense of purpose clearly has been there all along, but here it is, for real! And his empathy glowing and growing stronger. He is important to others and that is what counts in life. He has a wonderful Nana teaching him the true meaning of life. Not a car, not a part of town, not riches in the 'fancy' sense. Knowing life's beauty through rainbows, joy and love. And a giving heart.

Last Stop on Market Street offers us a lyrical, sweet bus ride into empathy. That last stop taught CJ the true meaning of life; humility and humanity. I'm certain he discovered hope, purpose, and a life filled with meaning. That last stop was his best, but the others prepared CJ for the ending, helping; really, just the beginning.

May we all find joys each day, as we continue to serve, just like Nana and CJ, every day…one way or another.

Leaving footprints on your reading hearts, Rita

7B

STATE OF THE DREAM IN THE NEW YEAR
January 14, 2017

Dr. Martin Luther King's birthday and ESSA, Every Student Succeeds Act.

With hope in my heart and passion in my soul, may we recognize Dr. King's aspirations and belief in the future success stories for all of America's children.

Tonight my heart is filled with joy. As we welcome successes of the New Year, I have faith in the future of our public schools. This is the perfect time to celebrate!

Dr. Martin Luther King's birthday, January 15th is here.

This date marks my birthday, and forty-sixth year as a teacher. It doesn't get better than that! And here I am, still teaching, now in a preschool, hopefully making a difference.

I was born on Dr. Martin Luther King's birthday. Perhaps that is why I have always had such a strong social conscience. I've been teaching reading nearly my whole life. When I was six, I was dragging neighborhood kids into my 'schoolroom.' Becoming a Principal was logical and a highlight of my career.

I was involved with literacy-related boards and organizations, including Literacy Volunteers of America, Neighborhood Study

Centers, Laubach Literacy, Homeless Coalition, etc. We walk in the footsteps of greatness, angels making a difference in the learning lives of children.

Dr. King, revered as a grand humanitarian, had a dream that all children have access to a great education and better world. Those aspirations hold true today.

About Title I, landmark act leveling the playing field. And ESSA.

I worked as a Title I program evaluator for many years. This has always been a great program, a landmark act dedicated to helping needy kids. The intent was to bridge the achievement gap between underachieving, underserved American schoolchildren.

For many years, money funded special teachers and programs, before, during, and after school. The sad news is the ethnic black-white gap has widened since No Child Left Behind (NCLB) with twelfth grade black children scoring lower in 2013 than 1992. Newest scores are not much better.

With so many schools under 'Improvement' status, and many states getting waivers, obviously there needed to be a rewrite of this legislation. It's always good to step back and see what's working and what's not.

And high stakes testing was not working to improve instruction. ESSA gives us a fresh start and new wave of academic optimism!

In my bleak moments I find myself dwelling on the poor test scores of our nation's children in reading. In particular, the realization that black children have not advanced, despite best intentions, due to a wide variety of factors, poverty being a big one, is heartbreaking to the core of my being.

Dr. King had a noble dream. We all share that dream. Every voice is significant. Great leaders excel in motivating excellence. And great leaders are everywhere.

Margaret Mead offered a favorite insight.

"Never doubt that a small group of thoughtful committed citizens can change the world. Indeed, it's the only thing that ever has."

Dream with Dr. King and me.

Dr. King's dream was, and is, achievable. It's the perfect time to help create capable students, in particular, confident readers and writers.

Teachers are so advanced in technology, even more important, the art and craft of teaching. It appears to me, this professional cadre is the most outstanding group of professional teachers, ever. Dr. King's dream is coming true, thanks to you!

What seems to matter most remains interdisciplinary curriculum, formative ways of measuring, direct experience with real life questions, and problems solved by applying skills across disciplines. Offering students leadership opportunities as learners, helps them make connections and builds self esteem.

The metacognition or 'thinking about thinking' modeled by teachers soon becomes a natural feature of student learning.

I believe that these elements are critical factors to achieving Dr. King's dream:

1. Create thoughtful curricular alignment with expected outcomes.
2. Find appropriate assessment tools to gather baseline data.
3. Determine what skills to teach next based on mastery and interest.
4. Instruct skills within targeted instructional strands.
5. Measure achievement with tools that assist instruction.
6. Offer teachers opportunity to determine their preferred pedagogy.

7. Put the money into classrooms, not testing.

Tremendously exciting, students as directors of their learning in student-centered classrooms, discover what they want and need to know. Teachers engage kids in a multitude of fantastic learning opportunities, unimaginable only a few years ago. We are entering the schools of the future right now, and that is certainly a good thing for all kids.

So I am totally optimistic we will succeed, Dr. King. Your dream is coming true. No matter what.

When Dr. King offered his wisdom and dream, we see his optimism, hear the fervor, and acknowledge the importance of his legacy.

My goal is to motivate and inspire you, shining a spotlight on literacy. Our hopes and dreams for children everywhere highlight the intense need, and efforts made by schools to meet and exceed the most humble goals, to the sublime.

Reading research is abundant. Best practices are research-based, evidence-driven and the product of tried and true, common sense classroom strategies modeled by coaches and teachers. If we truly are to become a nation of readers, let's continue highlighting what's working and replicate the best. This is happening now within our educational community, especially through social media.

I've never been more optimistic.

Every day we read stories of academic, intellectual bravery, and courage. Dr. King would be proud, I think, regarding the generosity of various literacy-based foundations and individuals contributing to the cause, in large, and small, worthy, noble acts.

There was the story of the barber who cut children's hair for free when presented good report cards. Stories of athletes and personalities donating books and backpacks to needy children. How about the librarians on bikes and book buses getting to kiddos who have no resources? I hope we can get more internet access to children.

Most obviously, teachers feed hungry children, buy classroom supplies and materials, Principals ensure children's basic needs are met and motivate and inspire school staff to continue professional learning.

It's true, test scores are not where they should be. If we get stuck that the achievement gap was not bridged and goals unmet, we negate the bright future promise of student achievement. Assuming it's true, 51% of public school children live in poverty and more are certainly on the edge, I believe schools are meeting the challenge admirably.

It is with the greatest respect tonight I thank America's school leaders for tackling daily challenges with grace and dignity. Teachers are creating wonderful classroom environments with little money, sometimes in small cramped spaces, and instructing haunting, hungry children yearning for stability.

Great principals share the vision, mission, and leadership. They create school cultures where all are heard and flourish. Loving teachers make a lifelong difference that cannot be measured by summative test scores.

We certainly are accomplishing what Dr. King hoped for. We may not be there yet, but are well on the way. Don't you agree?

Never give up! Dr. King wants us, I'm sure, to stand firm in our beliefs in what is right and true for kids.

Leaving footprints on your reading hearts, Rita

7C

Finding Love Again
December 11, 2016

Today is Human Rights Day.

Ironic we have to set aside a special day, when it should be the norm. Human rights for all. All the time.

We are Teachers. We are strong and mighty. It's time to find love again, doing whatever it takes. We're all in this together. Let our voices 'raise the roof.' We cannot sit idly by and watch divisive factors hurt our children. They are the core of our being as a nation and family.

Tonight I am writing from my heart and depths of my soul. I dedicate this missive to my unyielding belief in full inclusion and equity. We are one, deserving the rights and equal treatment accorded each of us alone, and as a united people. By law….and doing what's right.

The busy holidays also tear at us, feeling behind in life, yet enjoying the frenzy. Stomach flu, a cold or two, like coal in one's stocking. Inevitable. We are Teachers. We are strong and mighty.

What a week!

Finding it difficult to discern news anymore. Listening to 'Soundscapes,' watching movies…and reading a lot. Quiet.

Eugene is as diverse as diverse can be. Went to 'Ecstatic Dance' at the WOW Hall. Very Zen and calming in the turbulence.

Drank a lot of tea. Ate soup. Take out Thai. Pondered world events and mostly, public schools and their fate. The Homelessness here sucked at one's marrow, in unending rain every day. Cocooned. My daughter's car broke down and she walked home in freezing cold.

The Storm.

Summoned to my kids' house. Sleepover through blustery days has been such a respite and extraordinarily happy time with my kids, Morgan, and dogs. My side of Eugene has ice, a trade-off for deer eating the scant berries and turkeys strutting in my yard.

I live by beautiful trails where I walk Gus, my big, red, standard poodle. I meditate and calm myself. Torrential rains negated our special time.

Caught a cold, missed school, only worked one day; finished reading a novel, hung out on Twitter and Facebook. Mini-vacation!

Had an acupuncture treatment. Came to a halt. Watched nearly non-stop episodes of "The Queen" on Netflix.

Spent a lot of time with Go Noodle, dramatic play and reading with Morgan, a 'kinder.' She is still playing Teacher, just like I did, so not much to say about that.

Zipped through her school Seesaw posts, just wonderful! Great teacher. Kids are learning sign language, Spanish, and starting coding. They have tablets, and a plethora of stations and time to learn through developmentally appropriate play.

I am fascinated teaching Morgan, a lefty, how to form letters. Reading is clicking. She has an amazing library. I saved her mother's books just for her.

Signing holiday cards, placing stickers and stamps on the envelopes, counting and stacking was great practice. Morgan also got five dollars which she put in her cash register. She's using the money to have a family party Christmas morning and made up her invitations.

During my visit, Morgan taught me a variety of features on my phone and showed me how to use her Kindle. She almost found her house on Google Maps. Techie.

Thinking about my life.

I always reflect in December, thinking about the past year and all my years, my two conflicting sides, family—and flip side, educators and students. I'm a couple days into it right now. So far, so good... mostly.

I still can't fathom I ended up helping at preschool! My commitment's made, efforts strong and mighty. Getting up a 5:30 am not so great, but once I get to school, I am in a bliss state and any doubts vanish. I joined a fully-inclusive, multi-age school; diverse in nature, with human rights at its very core.

We are Teachers. We are strong and mighty!

The Election.

Didn't know whether the Department of Education would be dismantled, or gain a voucher proponent at top; found out that one really quickly.

Are we 'rearranging deck chairs on the Titanic,' or embarking on a completely different utopian course, future-ready with a brand new deck of cards?

- So many unknowns at the moment.
- Speaking as a forty-six-year teaching veteran, still with young children daily.
- Speaking as a mother and grandmother, aunt, sister, and friend.
- Speaking out because we must all speak out for Human Rights.
- Bullying and harassment are illegal under Title IX...and in a 'civilized' nation.

We are Teachers. We are strong and mighty!

Finding love again.

That's why we will succeed in the long haul: because together we find strength and mentors. When we doubt ourselves, others lift our spirits and help us re-connect.

We have our Vision and Mission and know there is no failure... only feedback.

Our belief that all children deserve a quality education is achievable, recognizing there are obstacles to overcome, one pebble at a time.

We are a large, mighty force. We are Teachers!

Each day we find love again when we see our children shine. We are mama and papa bears, protecting vulnerable youngsters. We have a 'duty to protect.' Resilience is one thing, but hunger is another. First and foremost, children of all ages must feel safe, at home, at school and out and about the world. It's up to us to make this a reality.

We are Teachers. We are strong and mighty!

Upgrade public schools, stop blame game.

- Fully fund public schools; not vouchers.
- Dump most standardized tests. Teachers know how to do formative and summative assessment. Put the money into classrooms.
- Give teachers freedom and confidence; they are consummate professionals and deserve respect.
- Lower class sizes. With more than 51% of America's children living in poverty, and more on the edge, schools must have money to work with...and fewer kids per teacher. It only makes sense.

We are all truly servant leaders, regardless of title and position. We serve extended families and the learning community. We are naturally humble, for in humility we have empathy with others, especially diverse students who learn in varying ways and amounts of time.

Teachers are so creative. Encourage cultural environments where teachers are unleashed and find the joy of innovation and exhilarating creation. Children are great learners.

Schools are families. Family is family.

When all is said and done, family is the most important thing. Most teachers at some time or other question school needs vs. quality home life. Trade-offs are in order. Prioritizing is so important. No regrets later. I have a life, yet I think about taking care of other kiddos and not being home for our four.

If we are indeed in a sort of technological, corporate revolution, it is inevitable that things are rapidly changing, minute-to-minute. And that is exhausting.

By focusing on school culture, climate, and morale, our 'school family' can weather any storm, find a port, and sail smoothly as possible. No anchors can hold us back.

Our 'home family' deserves us to be fully present also, this holiday season, putting aside our concerns and worries about the world around us. It is vital we relax, reflect, laugh, sing, dance, and hold one another tightly. And affirm our love for one another.

Finding love again may be at school in a tumultuous year, reveling in all the wonderful learning and learners, lessons that worked perfectly. Thanking ourselves for teaching hard-to-reach kiddos in our care and forgiving ourselves for one who ran away, couldn't engage—stuff beyond us.

We are Teachers. We are strong and mighty!

Love and humility

I think now that love is the deepest form of humility. When we truly commit to another or what we deem a just cause, our humanity beams brightly, a beacon to all.

As winter storms pound us to the core, those natural, and others people-created, may we remember the many blessings our professional calling continually offers, regain core values, strength, and tenacity to stand for what's right.

Great leaders exude love, encourage love, and model love. What we do, matters. When we work quietly and gently, in a whisper of excellence. When we lean a little. If cornered, play hard-core Jenga so tumbling pieces get righted in the jigsaw of school life.

Being humble servant-leaders guides us, drives us and puts protective white light around those in our care while we right the ship of excellence in 'The Perfect Storm.' This time we make it out. It is grand that we are almost on vacation break. This is such a fun time of year for kids...us too. Love the crafts, learning celebrations, and unfiltered joy. Bliss!

We are Teachers. We are strong and mighty! But we deserve a break...

The best part of the holiday season is leaving our cares behind; festive, musical, fun-filled time, and hopefully, time to rest. Then rejuvenate. This year I think we all deserve it.

Last night as winds howled and rains poured outside, inside our family decorated a beautiful tree, affirmed our holiday plans and played joyous holiday music, our bonds solidified.

Many blessings to you and your school and home families as the year draws to a close. Sending happy thoughts for a magical, carefree ending to the year and a toast to new beginnings! And on Human Rights Day, I thank you all for making a difference in the lives of children. What nobler cause could there be?

Leaving footprints on your reading hearts, Rita

7D

EVERYBODY COOKS RICE: LEARNING TO COOK TOGETHER
November 12, 2016

World Kindness Day.

I am writing this tonight from my heart. It's World Kindness Day today!

Recent events caused me to lose my faith for a bit. It wasn't just about who won or didn't win the election, but the level of hate spewing throughout…and continuing. I worry about the children affected, the intense divisions; yet hope our collective voices will shout what needs to be done, our collective actions will be wise and sure.

I pray we act through our conscience, regardless of our beliefs. Everyone is perfect in every way, even if we disagree on some things. Getting to 'Yes!' matters.

What we all must agree on is that it is our duty to protect our children. Our compassion comes before anything else right now until the ship rights itself and smoother seas prevail. While we are in unchartered waters as educators, parents, and members of the larger world community, let us find ways to serve our country and ensure all children are nurtured, treated equally, and receive a quality education.

That brings me to the extraordinarily beautiful, poignant in our time, classic, *Everybody Cooks Rice.* Read it. You'll get the connection.

I love this book! It's perfect for right now…maybe more than ever. Author Norah Dooley and illustrator Peter J. Thornton (1991) created a classic masterpiece of belonging, a simple neighborhood world where everyone lives close by, all get along, and commonalities far outweigh any differences.

Rich characters and illustrations provide a gorgeous example of multiculturalism. We meet families from other countries we can identify on a map as a mini-lesson, including Barbados, Puerto Rico, Vietnam, China, India, and Haiti. Launching off for great lessons and teachable moments.

I am sharing this beautiful book tomorrow at school. We are already learning book handling, concepts of print, sounds make letters, letters make words. My objectives are a little different.

First and foremost, I hope to encourage empathy and understanding we are all the same in our hearts and souls. Our 'littles' already understand 'inclusion' and 'diversity.'

We spend much of our teaching time modeling sharing and caring for each other. Resolving differences. Putting Band Aids on our boo boos. Saying "sorry," and cleaning up our messes. We are learning character; I am learning humility and peace.

Feeding our hungry students all day long; pulling zippers, putting shoes on right feet. In between I ask high-level questions, we cheer those who speak a first word and start stringing a sentence together... and ensure all are friends on the playground and no one gets picked on. Finding bugs and worms remains highest priority.

We are zooming on skills, too, helping the majority of kids who have unique ways of learning and really need to be taught only one-to-one to excel.

All the children are unique in every way, but they work in pairs, a 'big' and a 'little,' all day long...including getting ready for meals, mats ready, washing hands, and holding hands for safety.

I think about my own family. This year, we are more split up than usual, more apart than together, but clusters will be together in a couple of states. But when we all do sit together, I look around at an extraordinary family made up of a variety of religions, beliefs, and cultural backgrounds. We all get along and love each other madly. Just like our school. School and family are one. Seamless.

Family.

Everybody Cooks Rice is like my family. Maybe I just like to think so; I'm not sure. I do know that this sweet story is about family, first and foremost.

Here's the sequence. As Anthony goes on his nightly exploration up and down the street of what's for dinner, sister Carrie is supposed to track down her brother.

We first meet Mr. and Mrs. D. from Barbados. Grand tales, cooking with tumeric. Then looking for Anthony at Dong Tran's house. He's from Viet Nam. Fried rice, and peas, and more.

Maybe Anthony is at the Huas'. Well, how about Rajit's? Yum, biryani cooking, there. Oh, now at Hua's. Chopsicks, vegetables, and rice. The Bleus are cooking Haitian style including, you guessed it, red beans and rice.

Back at home, Mom learned from her Italian grandmother how to make a special rice-with-green-peas and is cooking up a tasty pot.

By this time, Carrie, having sampled the yummy rice dishes in her close-knit neighborhood, is too full to eat. But Anthony, a great neighborhood rice sampler, is always up for more rice. Because 'everybody cooks rice!'

My lesson plan for tomorrow, large and small groups.

- Wear my Chinese slippers and apron.
- Refer to world map and one of their favorite books about China, and it's big!
- Make predictions, what the book is about.
- Check out special features of the book through a Book Walk.
- Provide examples of our teamwork and belonging, as segue to story.

- Discuss helping brothers and sisters, and our friends at school.
- Dramatic play, act out story and its sequence.
- Fine motor skills: use chopsticks to pick up raisins.
- Kinesthetic: Salt trays for letters we have studied.
- Art and music: paint one scene or character.
- Maybe get out my rhythm instruments.
- Extension: Read recipes in the back of the book and see if I can cook it this week at home, then eat it at school. Rice, for sure!

Everybody Cooks Rice, a classic in belonging and empathy, nothing could be better for youngest kids.

I believe in you. May you be blessed by teaching children of all ages and stages.

There are many things not in our control right now, but a positive attitude, protecting those who need to be protected, and modeling a ferocity and intensity of 'Can do' spirit ensures the strength of our families, communities, and nation—the United States of America. God bless you all tonight.

Leaving footprints on your reading hearts, Rita

7E

LESSONS FROM GEESE, REVISITED:
LEADERSHIP AND LIFE
January 21, 2018

I've been hearing geese honk all day.

It seemed last night that they were louder than usual. Since moving by the river, I expected to hear the rapids, but I certainly didn't think I would be sitting reading, listening to geese honk! I'm never sure whether they are flying back and forth to the duck ponds across the road, or going home. Wonder where their home is? Are they local geese, Oregon geese, or are they from somewhere else? Do they look the same as the other geese? Do they speak the same goose language?

The other day I read geese fly home each year. I have that instinct too, since moving to Eugene. I wonder where these geese are going? I was used to seeing geese near my home in Northern California. I lived forty-five minutes from Lake Tahoe, in the middle of nowhere. Mountain life was so different than here in Eugene. But geese in both places were comforting as my life shifted dramatically.

Have you ever looked up and simply watched flocks of geese gliding above? We used to have a couple Canadian honkers that vacationed on our property from January to May each year. Our very own 'snowbirds'. We named them 'Edgar' and 'Matilda.' It was really funny. I didn't know geese had a personality and noisy voices. They had never been around that close, before. I knew they had a funny, nasty hiss when they were waiting for the corn bucket, or not getting their way. Just like couples everywhere, pretty much (and teams resolving conflicts, which are inevitable in transforming organizations and schools).

My husband and I put out cracked corn every day, a very big enticement for company, and sure enough, all of a sudden like clockwork, we'd hear the pair fly overhead, and land gracefully, skimming on our pond. Never was sure how they could spot that the corn was out, then circle back around.

They came for their daily visit, creatures of habit, so to speak, in rain, snow, ice; it never mattered. Except for us, gingerly wading through snow to get their treat out.

The geese had the same routine every day, pretty much. Came in, a lot of honking, like "we're here," swam and ate for awhile. Then sure enough, they would come out of the water, waddle around the pond (just like *Bears in the Night*), walk up the steep-ish hill, meander slowly toward the barn, check out the compost pile, then waddle over to the back yard behind our house looking for the cracked corn we put out.

It was fascinating how they teamed up. One goose ate while the other guarded. Usually Matilda ate first. Poor Edgar really sacrificed most of the time. Sometimes they wouldn't get along, but resolved their conflict after a little hiss, changing places, and some bobbing and weaving.

We know that geese mate for life.

When one of our pair was lost after a number of years, several interlopers attempted to get with the remaining goose, and take over the pond and grassy knolls for themselves. Finally, the remaining goose of the couple just disappeared. But the newer, younger pair who had already been warned away in a number of little skirmishes over a couple years, (actually several worthy-to-watch air, ground, and water skirmishes) just took over the yard as new-crowned royals.

It was a destination resort for our geese, with beautiful property to wander, the pond, plenty to eat, and areas to hide in; predators held at bay.

I spent a lot of time geese-watching, as well as other critter, including skunks, foxes, deer, bear, etc. Our large picture windows offered the best entertainment: animal spotting. It's how I got to know geese as splendid creatures, calming to watch, my Zen.

Each day, as twilight came in on tiny little feet, our residents reversed their course to fly home. I think they were back and forth, to and from Sly Park Lake, four miles from our historic home. But I am not sure. How were these geese so smart that they found our property and came every day for food and a leisurely, safe day? How did they keep their secret from all the 'ordinary' geese at that lake? Was I imagining it?

At the end of the day, Edgar and Matilda, away from their flock, on their own, seemed to know when it was time to leave. They marched back up the hill, stood in place at the top, back up by the barn, and bobbing in deference to each other, again shared leadership, who gets to fly out first?

One would get a little ahead, then the other would make wishes known, and the pair would shift places. It went on for quite awhile before finally honking, "Let's go!" and around the barn they flew, so majestically. (I presumed headed back to their flock.) I always wondered how well the rest of their group accepted them as they were so different from the rest…or were they, really?

It is so comforting to turn off the news, gaze at the river, measure moments in terms of rapids-watching. And then, with a steady honking, out of nowhere come those magnificent geese! There is the 'V' formation! Look at that strong leader out in front pacing the group, keeping the flock working in sync, just like schools and organizations.

The continuity of life is so calming, Zen-like. Geese will always find a new group and join the formation. They know how to be leaders and followers. Just like us. It's time for us to be the strongest leaders imaginable, to dance the dance of love, steeped in kindness, stepping on as few toes as possible, while gliding along the dance floor of life.

Bring on the Zen. We need to relax. Too much stress! Self-care is no joke. We need each other. Better together, just like the geese. I'm hearing them right now. They have been serenading me all day as I reflected on my peace.

This eloquent, classic leadership story is credited to several authors, but I'll go with Milton Olson's 1991 version. If you know it, I hope you share with others. It's so timely.

Lessons from Geese.

As each bird flaps its wings, it creates an 'uplift' for the bird following. By flying in a 'V' formation, the whole flock adds 71% more flying range than if each bird flew alone.

Lesson One: People who share a common direction and sense of community can get where they are going quicker and easier when they are traveling on the thrust of one another. Whenever a goose falls out of formation, it suddenly feels the drag and resistance of trying to fly alone, and quickly gets back in formation to take advantage of the 'lifting power' of the bird immediately in front.

Lesson Two: If we have as much sense as a goose, we will stay in formation with those who are headed where we want to go. When the lead goose gets tired, it rotates back into the formation and another goose flies at the 'point' position.

Lesson Three: It pays to take turns doing the hard tasks and sharing leadership, interdependent on one another. The geese in formation honk from behind to encourage those up front to keep up their speed.

Lesson Four: We need to make sure our 'honking from behind' is encouraging, helpful, constructive, and supportive. When a goose gets sick or wounded, or shot down, two geese drop out of formation and follow him down to help protect him. They stay with him until he is either able to fly again, or dies. Then they launch out on their own with another formation or to catch up with the flock.

<u>Lesson Five</u>: If we have as much sense as the geese, we'll stand by each other and help each other, just like that.

Lessons from Geese is simply timeless. An inspiring gift, it instinctively offers us lessons in leadership, cooperation, teamwork, and love. Geese certainly build capacity in their flock through constructs of their life. So...

Let's be Geese!

Leaving footprints on your reading hearts, Rita

CHAPTER 8

THE SCHOOLHOUSE, AND LIFE'S REAL LESSONS

Teacher as a Thought Leader: School and Life Lessons.

Chapter Eight treats you with forever-hot-topics. My thoughts on homework, textbooks, kindergarten suspensions, cursive writing, competition, and more. The home-to-school connection should be seamless and strong. Parents are in partnership with schoolhouses and have a lot to say about how things go down.

A) Take a Spring Textbook Walk! Or Not...
B) Redshirting K: "Yay" or "Nay?"
C) Butter Battle: Yooks, Zooks, and Kinder Suspensions
D) Cursive Writing: What's the Big Deal?
E) Homework: Yes, No, Maybe So?
F) Participation Trophies and Winning! What Do You Think?

8A

TAKE SPRING TEXTBOOK WALK! OR NOT...

May 6, 2017

Ditch the Books?

Textbooks. How old are yours? Is this the end of the 35-pound backpack, stuffed lockers, and the extinction of textbooks?

One school was in the news this past year. Apparently the administration, Principal and Assistant Principal, ordered a roundup of all the textbooks in the school, piled them up and away they went. They were believers in no textbooks—better use of technology. Not all teachers and students were too thrilled because they were not ready for such a drastic change, with no input or warning.

I just discovered our local school district is upgrading elementary and high school science curriculum and corresponding materials. Would you believe it's been nineteen years since an update?

I was shocked to learn the district had not upgraded its science curriculum for more than a decade! I guess I shouldn't be. I seriously doubt your school has all-new curricula for all grades, subjects; all new textbooks. How about iPads, tablets, and laptops for all students?

Textbooks? So expensive, may be biased, or not, already dated by the time they are in students' hands. Heavy-as-heck, so redundant. All those giant high school books could probably be whacked in half with proper editing. Textbook dollars could be redirected to new technologies.

And if there are multiple authors, it's not so easy to determine the author's writing pattern. With one author, the writing pattern provides easily recognizable, emphasis at top, middle, end or repeated. And plan to have the books for a number of years end up dog-eared and worn. Inevitable.

Obviously, it's fantastic news that our new local approval means an addition of earth science, overdue updates and, I imagine, a ton of revisions. Maybe Pluto will reappear. More in-depth, targeted science instruction. NGSS (Next Generation Science Standards) to meet. Real-life science as focal point: Science, Technology, Engineering, Math (STEM).

The high school version costs nearly $600,000, paid by a bond. Materials included in the new curricula include: combinations of traditional texts, online resource subscriptions, tech support materials, professional development, etc. Seems like a great combination!

I served as a Curriculum Developer and consultant for many years at County Office and State levels. Involved in adoptions; the multi-faceted layers of point/counterpoint took eons and was extremely frustrating at times. Getting to "Yes."

It is always critically important that all stakeholders have voices heard. Time, when the future is now, it's really iffy. Are we simply 'rearranging deck chairs on the Titanic?' Will traditional physical textbooks hang around much longer? Will digital learning completely replace 'old school' textbooks?

Educational leaders have to be smarter consumers of information than ever before. Digital learning materials are here to stay, and flourish. My bet is textbook publishers will stay in the game, profiting off a new wave of cutting-edge interactive software.

Time, money, in short supply. Mastery of current, relevant, content-specific, engineering (STEM), and 'crosscutting concepts,' mandated core knowledge with opportunity for electives. I see students better prepared for college or career.

In an era of 'building capacity' while 'working lean,' this never-ending debate whether to use textbooks or 'ditch the books,' may be at the forefront of our new learning.

After all, apps and websites are being consistently and continually updated. Textbooks are 'old as the hills' the minute they are printed. Might as well "Hey, Siri," or hit the search buttons. Wikipedia.

Locally, the Oregon State Department of Education adopted new science standards in 2014. Here we are four years later, biology to be added in a future year. The preparation work that was done was plentiful. Teachers field-tested, publishers did their usual; no different now than when I was Principal.

Why we need to keep textbooks...or do we?

1. How current are your textbooks?
2. Are there enough books for all students?
3. Do textbooks stay in classrooms or go home for homework?
4. Heavy to haul around? Have enough lockers?
5. How many teachers are proponents of skipping textbooks entirely, using technology and online resources?
6. Are staff members believers in 'Ditch Text?'
7. What is your opinion about using textbooks—or ditching books entirely?
8. If you are a proponent of keeping and actively using textbooks, what do you say to teachers who skip books?

Are you currently involved in textbook adoption?

There are certainly differing viewpoints about info-texts, and 'ditching textbooks' which may mean, a complete dumping of books, or a more gentle merging of books with technology and project-based learning activities.

One angle is the complete tossing out of books, in favor of technology. Mind you, I am fairly new to the world of technology. I still have my Mac tutor occasionally and truly, our 'kinder' is teaching me how to use new-to-me features on my phone.

I was raised with, and used only textbooks. I love learning about Google Docs, Kahoot, Flipgrid. Amazing, students can do podcasts, Google-based research papers, and more up-to-date reports with such precision, working in all kinds of team situations. Critical thinkers; mindful learners with intention.

Raised with technology, today's students have a distinct advantage. Catching up is way harder and like rolling the wheel up the hill. Our 'kinder' is already learning coding and she goes to a technology-based school.

So I am not writing as expert of technology; expert on textbooks, probably yes. And today, I am reconsidering what I have always thought about the importance of 'physical' textbooks for kids.

More relevant, creative lessons are what we all talk about. I see a natural evolution, if not revolution, against the use of textbooks. We need to listen to teachers.

Real-life, project-based, both teacher- and student-initiated lessons may be of greater interest and definitely student-centered. Mindful, purposeful teaching, with questions as the center of discovery.

Truthfully, I can't imagine any teachers doing only direct-instruction, solely lecture-based, textbook-centered; no matter how excellent anymore. My ideal is blended-learning, inquiry-anything, project-based learning; high-interest, high-tech, real-world, useful-everything learning. Teacher on the side works perfectly for me, orchestrating a symphony-of-flow state. Whatever works—just do it.

Discussions of room arrangements, flexible seating, concepts of homework and grades; there's nothing new here. Now textbooks, that greatly concerns me. However, using old books certainly cannot advance our children to world-class standards.

Throw in poverty and a lack of internet access into the mix, plus shortage of funds; bulky textbooks, out of date. Teachers supplying materials and resources out of pocket, scrounging for donations for classroom technology, dealing with large class sizes. Meeting needs, differentiating everything. What a challenge! Our children deserve better.

Textbooks cost a lot of money that could be used for other purposes…maybe. And then we talk about Finland, and its high literacy rate, for goodness sakes.

If you are using textbooks, as a base or adjunct to your instruction:

1. Why use textbooks? (Launching off point.)
2. Excellent for new teachers, in most cases.
3. Builds 'schema,' or background knowledge.
4. Offers a chronological sequence, or roadmap for course syllabus.
5. If students do not have internet access at home textbooks become invaluable.
6. Advantages and disadvantages and how to overcome.

There is no reason why textbooks can't be used in conjunction with digital learning. 'Blended learning' is the best example, with textbooks as an adjunct print resource to open source and other digital platforms.

Today I thank you all for your devotion to the best education possible for all students—with or without textbooks.

Leaving footprints on your reading hearts, Rita

8B

REDSHIRTING K: "YAY" OR "NAY?"

April 29, 2017

What's the rush? Childhood is a precious time!

'Redshirting.' Not just in athletics. The competition is fierce... in kindergarten! I have mixed emotions. It's way more common than I thought and it actually affects all of us, all grade levels. What a big decision. It's more than birthday cut-off-dates, or maturity. In some cases it gives a step up to catch up; it can also be used to get to the 'top of the pack,' the delay adding a distinct advantage.

In our preschool, kids are definitely ready for kindergarten. The 'fives' are showing their muscle and I notice a lot more chasing on the play areas. Less looking for worms and snails; more boo boos.

Academically, kiddos are in touch with the world, know "please" and "thank you," clean up their messes, and can sing the names of all the states (thanks to Teachers Cheryl and Tom). I really don't get any credit, believe me. Teacher Tom has taught the children sign language. There's no end to this simply extraordinary program.

I've been asked to come back and help for another year. Yes, of course for the 'littles,' but next year even littler: mostly two-to-five-year-olds, littler than little. It took me all year to master our teachers' routines, learn how to do even the most simple crafts. I have to make a model of everything, first. Teacher Cheryl simply throws a bunch of odds and ends together, everything looks awesome.

I am learning how to teach all over again.

It's really no different than any other grade or content level I've taught, Kids are kids. And at least most of the time these kiddos get to learn through play. The way it used to be before 'bubbling in' came to pass. And a lot of other stuff that simply made no sense to me. How can you script kids?

I spend a lot of time saying "anybody gotta' go potty?" And I teach, even while children are standing in line to wash their hands, which is frequently.

Such a glorious experience. Instead of just writing about it, I am doing it. Not just as a volunteer, like I started a few times during Summer Camp, but now I'm at school, hopefully helping. I pour (and spill) a lot of milk.

Lookin' good, almost final concert tap-dance-ready.
(No credit to me.)

- ABCs: can say, sing and write. Multi-sensory.
- Phonemic awareness, concepts about print, book handling. Ta dah!
- Left and right. No comment. So redundant!
- Resolve conflicts. A lot of tears. A lot of hugs. "I'm sorry."
- Children love school. Heartwarming.
- Our world is a wonderful place.

I know where they live in the larger world around them. Because of my full immersion into the world of the youngest, I readily change my thinking about things I thought I knew and understood.

In fact, I think I have changed my mind about 'kinder redshirting.'

At least now I am more open to the idea. When kindergartens lost their pianos, and play turned into masses of worksheets and assessment, things simply changed…and I don't think for the better.

Dick and Jane had ponies in every yard, a little much, but that isn't the way it is now, anyway.

With so many of our beautiful children living in poverty, and unknowns about continued lunch and afterschool programs (maybe breakfast too), poverty is rearing its ugly head. Poverty is the defining factor in most academic areas, especially literacy.

Unless qualified and able to attend a Head Start program, many families simply can't afford a quality preschool, unless we as a nation prioritize Universal Preschool, which I have been advocating.

Recently I read in *Education Week* and NPR that New York state is adding three-year-olds to its preschool program for four year olds. Priorities. That should be our model, at least for now.

Gift of Time: Maybe a great idea for some kids.

'Redshirting' may mean the gift of time. Maybe for some kids that gift of time is needed. Perhaps if a child is truly not ready for the intensive demands now placed on kindergarteners, it might be better than retention after the kindergarten year. Just exploring here. I have no firm convictions anymore. Youngest kiddos in a kindergarten class may be ready…or not. It just depends.

Dick and Jane had it going. Kindergartens were' kinder gardens.' I applaud America's early child educators who manage to keep the joy in, while balancing needs and demands. Today's kindergarten, as far as literacy, teaches what 'firsties' used to know and do. Insightful. Kindergartens are not what they used to be.

A young child, smart and full of joy, may not be ready for such heavy academic content. If play is not top priority, school will be joyless. As for the teacher, children who missed earliest experiences in preschool, are not starting at the same point; at the same time academic expectations are higher than ever. This is stressful and burning out some of our finest teachers.

Technically, I could say 'redshirting' is a retention. When I was principal, we had a fantastic pre-first, 'Junior Kindergarten' which propped students up, whether due to age, immaturity, or missing preschool. Our district stopped the program, saying it was retention.

It catches up, grade-to-grade when children were not ready. Then comes third. Too many children are retained in third grade. By third, kiddos are supposed to know how to read…in order to read to learn, in fourth.

I read Michigan and other states may be considering this cut-point again (in order to boost test scores, probably). It's ineffective for children, possibly devastating, and costs more money for another year of schooling. I am adamantly opposed to this practice!

That being said, at least three percent, or maybe five per cent or more of kiddos are being 'redshirted.' Google search and you'll find stories of both pros and cons. I had no idea so many people are even considering, well that's not quite accurate, just surprising the amount now. I get it.

More affluent parents have the option of paying for another year of a private preschool. What about children in poverty who have no opportunity to attend such a school? Does this give some children an advantage that lasts the rest of their life, including the workplace?

Tonight I am not quoting statistics, simply suggesting this time of year, as we look at what kindergarteners are expected to know and do both physically and mentally, perhaps the idea of redshirting may have some merit after all.

Kindergarten sign-ups have consequences. I've seen children start, then leave right away. I've also experienced frazzled teachers caught off guard. Some inexperienced kiddos are new to school and a lot more time has to be spent on basic routines.

Teachers can handle anything, but it is tiring to have a bunch of kids throwing themselves on the floor in a tantrum. This is reality. High expectations for youngsters may add unneeded stress. What are politicians and 'decision-makers' thinking? What's the rush?

My blog post on kindergarten suspensions adds a little more grist to the hopper. Is there a connection between more immature children who needed the extra year to get kindergarten ready? I don't know. What about 'redshirting?' Maybe a stop sign? Check out the kindergarten curriculum before making that BIG decision.

Leaving footprints on your reading hearts, Rita

8C

BUTTER BATTLE: YOOKS, ZOOKS & KINDER SUSPENSIONS

March 16, 2016

Dr. Seuss wrote *The Butter Battle Book* in 1984.

It is timely today, maybe more so. The story is about resolving differences, although in the book there is a background threat of mutual destruction, with an uncertain ending. A wall divides two groups, Yooks and Zooks simply because of the way they butter their bread. Isn't that just so Dr. Seuss?

This is a very different Dr. Seuss book, an anti-war story more suited to older students. However, I think adaptable to youngest children, and outrageously great for dealing with the problem of bullying at school. I recently read parts of it to my granddaughter, Morgan, as example of the silly things kids (and grownups) do when they have disagreements. (Her favorite book right now is the classic *Yo! Yes?* by Chris Raschla. In this joyous little story two kids realize they are lonely and decide to become friends.)

Childhood is such a precious time, our pre-kindergartener was pretty surprised that the Zooks and Yooks couldn't just figure it out, tear down that wall dividing them, and be friends with a happy ending just like *Yo! Yes?* Kiddos make life pretty darn simple when we watch and listen to them, don't you think?

Morgan and I made a Venn diagram, with *Yo! Yes?* in the middle. On one side, The Yooks wear blue clothes and eat their bread with butter side facing up. On the other part of the diagram the Zooks wear orange clothing and they butter their bread with the butter on the bottom. Of course, I didn't deal with anything more grown up than the basics and we had a fun time talking, drawing, and making our comparisons. Morgan had no idea she was doing critical thinking and we were asking questions based on Bloom's Taxonomy of higher-order thinking skills.

This leads me to making the connection with kindergarten suspensions.

It's really about Zooks and Yooks, when you think about it. No easy answers, just more and more questions.

I rarely suspended a student I thought was better off at home than school. In most cases, an in-house suspension or alternate work project (early version of PBL, Project Based Learning) style of discipline worked. There are often better ways to work with a misbehaving kid than suspension.

I read recently that more black and Hispanic children are suspended than statistically probable. That scares me, because in my recent NAEP blog, ("The Nation's Report Card"), I reported extremely low reading proficiency scores for black students at fourth and eighth grade. Not much better, at the fourth grade level; about one third of NAEP kids scored at the basic reading level.

That means there are lots of left-behind kids, despite schools' best, bravest efforts under daunting circumstances (and greatly underfunded). I wonder whether aggressive tests are creating aggressive kids?

Since 51% of America's pubic school children live in poverty, with more on the edge, I also wonder: is there a correlation between suspension and highly stressed students, one hundred thirteen standardized tests, loss of recess, arts, music and play due to the race to the top?

Why in the world do we have to be compared to Finland and Korea, when the best and brightest teachers and great leaders are right here, right now? Amazing technology, top-notch pedagogy or strategies, professional development, research, and authentically-based assessments tell us what to do to engage kids. Besides art and craft, head and heart take center stage in America's great classrooms. Engaged kids generally do not misbehave; so we have to take a closer look.

Temper tantrums? Chair-tossing, striking a classmate or teacher. I've seen it all and except for issues with teachers, there were always better ways for the 'punishment to fit the crime.' That's my point. The schools with high suspension rates happened to be in Georgia… but maybe where you teach or live, too. Hundreds of kindergarteners from the four largest districts were suspended. I weep for the teachers as well as the kids.

When I was a pre-K-6 principal, (two schools, one large campus) there were children who cried the first week or so, lacked social skills, and were fairly obnoxious. Goes with the territory. Considering I started my career as a high school English and Speech then Reading, teacher I saw the world a little differently, I think.

During my first week as a novice administrator, a kindergartener was so disruptive in the classroom I was pretty shocked. I recall the student throwing furniture, knocking over shelves and bookcases, etc. When I took him to my office for a cool-down, he did the same thing there. But I didn't suspend him for any of the havoc, lost instructional time, or frayed nerves. I got to the root of the problem.

Before I arrived, the school culture was grim. For example, boxing gloves were used to resolve problems. Teachers also paddled children, as did the principal. The assertive discipline program in place sent kids to the office in a steady stream, all day long, preventing any genuine leadership.

My point is, been there, done that. I know the difficulties experienced by frazzled teachers who truly have tried everything, including parent meetings, school intervention programs, whatever counseling is available, and home visits. However, nothing in my career prepared me for an article I read in the *Atlanta Journal-Constitution,* regarding the uptick in kindergarten suspensions.

About those suspensions.

Let's chat a little about the article's major points about management and misbehavior, as I understand them:

1. Parents or caregivers want their children in a nurturing classroom.
2. Administrators' number one responsibility is providing a safe and orderly environment.
3. Developmentally appropriate pedagogy is imperative for young children.
4. Play and recess are critically important. Brain breaks are great, but kids need to frolic.
5. At what cost has the rush to excellence stressed out our young kiddos?
6. Parents are our Partners. Any programs and home visits making a seamless bond, work.
7. School-wide culture of positivity only makes sense. POPS. Power of positive students.
8. Retentions at any level, notably pre-K, better have a really valid reason. Loathe the idea.
9. Are more black and Hispanic children suspended?
10. Are hunger and/or deprivation a mitigating factor in misbehavior?
11. Do Morning Meetings make a difference in setting the tone and resolving problems?

12. Are team projects and collaboration, including K level, helping kids learn to get along?

Why are kiddos so stressed, angry, acting out, mimicking violence? What are appropriate ways to help children see and experience logical consequences for their actions? What can we do to reach and help these children?

I ask you tonight how we can help keep so many children, at such a tender age, from becoming a statistic. Right now, hundreds (maybe a whole lot more) of kindergarteners are already a statistic, a suspended one.

Leaving footprints on your reading hearts, Rita

8D

CURSIVE WRITING: WHAT'S THE BIG DEAL?

January 26, 2016

I never thought this would be a big topic, but it is.

Today I'm making a brief comment about Cursive Writing, or lack of, in schools. Along with homework, this topic appears to be in a growing debate. With time scarce and deep, rigorous knowledge standards at the forefront of education (and rightly so) cursive writing has taken a big hit. Teachers and parents are truly caught in the middle. Opponents and proponents each make an eloquent case for their belief. And that's just fine. Let the debate begin.

In the meantime, I want to weigh in on the subject. I wonder how you feel about this. If you are a teacher, do you have time allocated in your curriculum to practice handwriting? If so, how much time do you spend? Are students only printing (or typing), or are they encouraged to write in cursive?

What's the big deal with cursive writing?

Nearly every day I read an article lamenting the loss of cursive writing. Perhaps you've seen various Facebook posts showing student papers coming home marked, "Stop writing in cursive." Why? I find this difficult to comprehend. And not all assignments can be done by keyboarding. What do you think about this?

I agree it's important for children to learn typing and keyboarding skills. This is obviously, a digital age in America. But typing and keyboarding are certainly different than the motor skills involved in handwriting. Fine motor skills combine with movement. Beautiful cursive is an art form, in my opinion. Cursive writing beautifies the written word and is a lost art. Fine motor skills are needed by young children—and writing contributes to fine motor growth.

Common Core did not focus on cursive writing, except an honorable mention in kindergarten and first grade. That made no sense to me, if accurate. When I teach the alphabet and basic writing, I start in block manuscript, of course, teaching by pointing out sticks, tunnels, circles and curves in letters. Moreover, I always advocate teaching upper- and lower-case letters at the same time, so a student can see that an 'A' is an 'a,' whether in upper or lower case. I move to cursive when the child has mastered basic manuscript. Cursive writing generally is taught by second or third grade, depending on school curriculum and state standards. It is certainly not measured on a standardized test.

Some years back, we saw growth of 'D'Nelian' handwriting. All over America, letters posted in wall charts around classrooms featured the switch from block to D'Nelian. It was thought that the letter curves in D'Nelian were a natural, viable link directly into cursive writing. Ironic, because manuscript or block printing more closely matched the letters in books, upper and lower case. D'Nelian was a derivative of what was known as the *Palmer* method and was thought to be the 'natural way' to teach handwriting.

I recall regular sessions for practicing cursive when I was a child in school. I loved forming the letters and sentences. My writing was quite beautiful then. Over the years, I wrote countless cards and letters; of course my signature on documents was always written in cursive.

Nothing matched my mother's writing.

Unreal, but I still have a copy of her *Berry's Writing Book,* 1909. In her practice book, pages and pages were devoted to forming perfect circles, lines, curves, letters, and ultimately sentences and paragraphs, in natural progression. All that practice made a difference. Today, the amount of time spent would be simply unimaginable.

As my kids grew up I noticed less and less cursive; more printing in manuscript, followed by typing and keyboarding. As a computer literate generation focused on laptops and tablets, the demise of cursive was imminent.

In her book, *What If Everybody Understood Child Development?* author Rae Pica has a chapter called, "Should We Teach Handwriting in the Digital Age?" Pica believes it's more than nostalgia, rather a necessary component of gross and fine motor development and offers compelling rationale for continuing this instruction in the Common Core era. I strongly encourage you to read her book and this persuasive chapter.

I can't imagine a time when children no longer know how to write in cursive. It is not only beautiful, but a developmentally appropriate practice for young children. People are indeed talking about it. I have no answers today, only more questions.

Leaving footprints on your reading hearts, Rita

8E

HOMEWORK: "YES," "NO," "MAYBE SO?"
November 15, 2015

How do you feel about homework?

I read an interesting article recently about parents threatening to leave their school when it stopped giving homework. Take a look at what happened. The school principal and teachers were concerned too many children were missing recess (scant to begin with) because homework wasn't done, which initiated the chain of events. (Obviously recess should not be used as a punishment anyway.)

The decision was well-considered. The Pre-K-5th School Council, including parents, thoroughly studied homework research. The findings of their homework committee, after a year of studying homework effectiveness, prompted the principal to decide that children should go home and play, spend time reading, and have family time instead of traditional worksheets and homework. The school found no significant research that warranted the continuation of a policy that wasn't working for their students.

I'm sure when they opted for developmentally-appropriate-play (DAP) and more reading, they never dreamed it would become a hot topic on Twitter and in the news media.

While I was a principal (K-6), we frequently reviewed homework policies, including parents in the discussions. After all, parents are monitors, tutors, and wipers-of-tears from a frustrated child. Homework varies school-to-school and teacher–to-teacher.

Many parents think that there is too much homework cutting into limited family time. Parents worry their child is overworked and discouraged. Other parents want homework, the routine of it, having a goal, working toward a reward, seeing what is learned at school.

Here are my thoughts:

'Teaching for transfer' means students take learning from one context to another. It makes sense to immediately review important concepts taught during the school day, then apply them in new ways. The value of homework is that lesson extension, with developmentally-appropriate engaging activities cements the new learning. *Flashbulb memory* occurs when an idea or event is so strong you remember it forever. Otherwise, some form of review and repetition is necessary to make the learning stick. Practice makes permanent.

Psychologist Hermann Ebbinghaus hypothesized that the greatest rate of forgetting occurs within twenty-four hours (*Ebbinghaus Forgetting Curve*) and recommended frequent review to retain memory. This may mean some homework can help students retain what they just learned.

How much homework? What kinds?

How much, and what type of study, matters. Why do twenty math problems, if five will reinforce the concept taught? For emerging readers, avoid busy work worksheets on paper (or online) which use nonsense words, scrambled words, or word searches. Use only correct models.

Teacher-created activities, and assignments that match, reinforce and extend what was instructed work best. Homework can offer enjoyable family activities and short-term projects which complement daily learning. Parents should read with their children at least twenty minutes a day, long—past toddler lap-reading. Less homework means more family reading time, sharing classic novels, and interesting internet articles. Schools can incorporate family reading time into their homework plan.

Online research about homework varies from a stance of no homework, to must-do homework, and how to make it really meaningful. If you have concerns about best meeting your child's needs, work with your teacher.

Suggestions for teachers:

- Homework should be at the *application* level.
- Apply what you've learned to new information.
- Be realistic about the amount of time it will take students to compete the assignments.
- Can the students do the homework alone, or are parents needed to tutor?
- How do you reconcile the fact some students won't get it done on any given day?
- How do your assignments developmentally help review and extend the new concepts?
- Make sure the work is done correctly at school.
- Have students check each other's work.

Suggestions for parents:

- Allow your child a brief time to play, snack, drink plenty of water—and take a breath.
- Start homework before dinner, not after. The learning must be fresh for the review to stick. Have a regular routine you consistently follow.

- Make a homework 'center' in your home, with proper lighting, seating, and supplies.
- Set a timer, or establish the amount of time homework should take.
- Take short breaks.
- If your child hits a frustration level consistently, talk with the teacher.

It seems to me that pulling a child out of school because of a no-homework policy is really drastic and non-productive. As a parent and a nana, I spent plenty of time with my own frustrated kids struggling with enormous amounts of homework. And that's not pretty.

But no homework at all? That swings a bit far for me. Personally, I know it's important to do quick reviews after the school day as long as there is purpose and meaning, it meets students' needs and interests, and it makes sense. Homework standards endorsed by the NEA (National Education Association) and National PTA (Parent-Teacher Association) suggest no homework for kindergarten.

Here are their time allocations (10-minute rule per grade level) for us to consider:

- 10 minutes for first grade
- 20 minutes for second grade
- Up to 120 minutes for high school seniors

There are many teachers and parents wanting to dump homework entirely who don't agree with this.

I've been reading that homework is probably at least three times as much as the suggested standards, but I really have no clue if that's true. In fact, I am weighing the homework debate very carefully. With school bells ringing, poor test scores causing finger pointing and wagging tongues, this is one debate we all better chime in on. Our home life and seamless extension with schools depends on it.

Should schools give homework? If so, what kind and how much?

Leaving footprints on your reading hearts, Rita

8F

PARTICIPATION TROPHIES AND WINNING! WHAT DO YOU THINK?

October 4, 2015

Change-of-pace consideration via a thought-provoking article.

I was in the middle of reviewing half a dozen blogs about teaching reading. One from HuffPost on Facebook caught my eye. I think it will generate a great discussion with your friends, family, and colleagues. Be sure to ask your own kids what they think about it, too!

If you saw the movies, "Meet the Parents" and "Meet the Fockers," you undoubtedly recall the scene where Gaylord's parents made a giant shrine of his participation ribbons and awards. He was not happy it was shared with his bride-to-be and her parents...but we all laughed and laughed, as everyone can relate.

The article I read was about an NFL star, linebacker James Harrison, who took away his two sons' 'participation' trophies. As a member of the Pittsburg Steelers, Mr. Harrison is an athlete, champion, and a winner. However, he opens up an interesting conversation for us with his actions as a sports hero and a parent. I am not judging, as he makes a valid point about earning awards and rewards.

James Harrison came up the hard way; super-stardom eluded him, and he worked passionately to overcome many obstacles to become a champion athlete. I admire that drive.

Competition, awards assemblies, and more...

As our school year starts, there are ramifications for classrooms and whole schools regarding 'awards assemblies,' grades, and competition of many sorts. School culture determines what values are most important and not everyone always agrees.

I don't believe in buy-in. But I do believe in civil conversation and ultimately doing what's best for children. My kids were champion swimmers and all-around athletes in many sports. (Not from my genes). Not all of our children excelled at the same things, but my husband, William, and I always celebrated their successes whether on the field, ski slope, pool, or classroom.

One of my step-kids is a champion climber. She never needed a 'participation trophy' or ribbon. Our other three were great at various sports and extracurricular activities, but perhaps may have been given a participation ribbon or trophy at one time or another growing up. I wonder if they kept them? I need to ask.

We attended countless practices, games, and meets regardless of win or loss. William also coached several sports he was not as experienced with because someone had to do it for the kids. He modeled good values and tenacity, which I think are more important in life than always winning.

It was all about the games, learning about teamwork, being a good sport, and sticking it out. The scores really didn't matter. And for those kids who were top athletes and got the accolades, super, but at least the other kids were recognized and felt pretty great about themselves. Talk about a 'growth mindset.'

I truly admire Mr. Harrison for his beliefs that his kids have to earn respect and be true champions to earn recognition. But I don't agree that his kids needed to lose awards. It's just my opinion.

Not every child is a super-star athlete; there will undoubtedly be a spectrum of excellence in life. That's what it's all about. By giving our kiddos lots of opportunities in a variety of areas, something always stands out.

My life work is all about reading.

I like to think I was a sometimes a champion as a parent, principal, and other things I did in my life. At least, I gave it my 'all.' In fact, my last book, *Reading Champs,* is about anyone coaching someone else, adult or student, to be a champion reader.

For me, teaching the skills necessary for academic- and life-success starts with our modeling. And that is the question I am posing. What are the values we impart as parents and caregivers? Is winning all that matters? Does participation and making a solid effort count?

I question whether taking back children's awards is the best way to model good sportsmanship. I would have applauded them for participating whether the team won or not. What does a child have to do to earn an award?

What do you think? Differing opinions are good. I am open to discussion. Perhaps I'm wrong. I surely hope so.

Leaving footprints on your reading hearts, Rita

Epilogue

On Optimism

The Teacher as an Optimist

Surviving

As a cancer survivor, I can assure you that the only thing that saved me was a small voice inside of me that suddenly started screaming, "Life is worth the effort!"

I wanted to live for granddaughter Morgan's wedding. I wanted to be at all our grandkids' weddings, too.

Her little hands, smiling face, and voice gave me strength when there was none. Only my optimism remained during daunting times and a life beyond what I could endure. My natural optimistic spirit shone through when I thought there was nothing left but hope. I gave up.

Find one thing today to focus on, see its beauty, savor the energy and I promise you that commitment makes the difference in a gracious life worth living, no matter what.

Rita Wirtz
October 12, 2018

Afterword

On Optimism, Lost and Found.

Simply too much going on to keep up with. Overwhelming!

I only write when I have something to say, or something to share. Lately, I am writing in my head, constantly. I'm barely sleeping. If I watch any news, or read the news on my phone, that's it for me.

Boing, I'm awake and fretting, restless, wandering around cleaning my closet or drawers and making notes for my book in progress, on little scraps of paper and pads left around.

What should I be focusing on? Where's my balance? Endless lists of to-do, overdue. My health worries, medical bills, paperwork piles, that sort of stuff. Add the fact I need to get my Oregon Drivers' License in a month, and I am already freaking out and test-phobic about not passing.

Add more to Strega Nona's pot, too many Big Anthony people running around messing up for others, not really listening and certainly not caring. The restless and not so restless winds of change in our country and political process, lack of civility, and no seeming knowledge how to get to yes anymore.

The enormous tragic losses of people from a myriad of causes. Floods, the storms, the horrendous fires, the relentless din of angry people and seemingly unsolvable problems. Shootings, homelessness, drug addiction, etc., etc. How in the world do we stay optimistic in a turbulent time?

No way to begin to categorize my distresses, and likely in some cases, yours, too. One either has some information, too much information or like me, sometimes just turning everything off, which doesn't solve anything, but helps our mental health, for sure. The roar of anger uncorked, venomous conflict over things we should be able to agree upon. It still makes no sense to me, the continual big news, not so big news and distractions.

Daily challenges of life, swirling events surrounding us. Hold tight.

I am the first to admit I lost my best, most optimistic self this past year. At least for a lot of the time, with some glimpses, maybe of the best me. On November 15, 2017, my late husband's milestone birthday, I got the dreaded doctor phone call. I was leaving preschool. Littles were napping, I had said "good-bye, see you tomorrow," gathered my book bags, disappeared in the art room with Teacher Cheryl, and cried, in shock and disbelief.

Other than a few visits, I was unable to return to teaching until last May, a month before the end of school. But yes, I did finish strong and it was a great way to celebrate my survival, hopefully make a difference in the learning lives of the littles I was privileged to teach.

And then, most unhappily I didn't return to every day teaching in September, instead planning to write a couple books, including my Memoirs, because I honestly didn't think I was going to make it. Rebuilding my health became my only goal, in my most optimistic moments. Not very optimistic, though. Until very recently I had a myriad of complications, like peeling the onion, and truly was not sure what it meant to be a survivor, even though I said it a lot.

Passion, purpose, courage, hope. Optimism means family first.

I have a large extended family, but everyone is spread out now, which is not what I envisioned. Because I moved several times to make this happen, first from California, then a couple times here in Oregon, I am now about ten minutes from my Eugene family.

I wish I lived by all our kids and their kids. I notice our grown children each living lives of passion, purpose, courage and hope. We raised them to be optimistic, to see only the good, do only the good and be the best possible in life, in whatever chosen path.

What is an optimist? How do we stay optimistic? Those defining moments.

For me, family and teaching provide the defining moments I savor and crave, too. I look for the people around us making a difference, standing up for beliefs, showing courage, fortitude, overlapping with tenacity. No matter what happens, the optimist finds the silver lining. Turns those proverbial lemons into lemonade. Makes those boulders to climb over or get around seem like little pebbles.

What purpose, passion, courage drives us to fruition when we feel we are beyond endurance? Servant leaders are often pushed to the limits, but courage shines through. What if we reframe the tragic events to a culture of coming together, opportunity, rebirth and renewal? I see this happening already. People are resilient, do not give up. Talk about optimism.

What if we come together as families, friends, communities and the larger world to solve problems we regard as vital opportunities? If we can't fix everything, what can we fix? What, as our most optimistic selves can we do to effect change, growth and transformation in ourselves and others?

I do believe we all have defining moments in our lives, whether joyous, such as rituals and celebrations, sudden illness, loss and other commonalities to the human condition. We are all one, sharing our hopes, dreams, aspirations and managing or hopefully beginning to find a balance between hard and not so hard, more beautiful vistas in our lives.

It is imperative we remain optimistic and not give in to fear, to share our moral courage and recognize together is better. Love is better than hate, surely, when all is said and done. We can certainly spread kindness and love.

I know I should, but even after all these years I still don't have that many answers about a lot of truly important things. I know I am an imperfect person, but I give my all, and have, my whole life.

I never thought I would lose my optimism even for a second.

I have many lists of beautiful personal affirmations I hold dear, but I think sometimes, even with the best of intentions, our better selves go awry under constant bombardment, maybe seemingly from all sides. I stayed pretty much in a dark hole for awhile, but coming back into the light is a really genuine expression of love and joy, which I am hopefully spreading to others.

By sharing and celebrating all the good we see every day, taking time to be in nature, forgiving those who have hurt us, and finding our depths of humility and gratitude, our grace and dignity shine through, and our most optimistic, souls.

Giving thanks tonight, my gift to you, 'The Optimist Creed.'

Promise Yourself:

- To be so strong that nothing can disturb your peace of mind.
- To talk health, happiness, and prosperity to every person you meet.
- To make all your friends feel that there is something in them.

- To look at the sunny side of everything and make your optimism come true.
- To think only of the best, to work only for the best, and expect only the best.
- To be just as enthusiastic about the success of others as you are about your own.
- To forget the mistakes of the past and press on to the greater achievements of the future.
- To wear a cheerful countenance at all times and give every living creature you meet a smile.
- To give so much time to the improvement of yourself that you have no time to criticize others.
- To be too large for worry, too noble for anger, too strong for fear, and too happy to permit the presence of trouble.

(Optimist International, Christian D. Larson, 1912.)

Closing Thoughts from my dear friend, author Robert Ward:
"Let's continue to move forward with:

- Faith: A deep trust in our own strength and an optimism that everything is going to work out great.
- Grace: Experiencing all things (good and bad) with calm composure and dignity.
- Gratitude: Focusing on the good and the positive all around us and turning our gratitude into acts of appreciation (paying things forward)."

From my head, heart and soul tonight,

Leaving footprints on your reading hearts, Rita

Bibliography of Classic Children's Books

All of Dr. Seuss books.

Amelia Bedelia (41 Books), Peggy Parish, 1963-88; Herman Parish, 1995-2015.

Are You My Mother?, P. D. Eastman, 1960.

Bear Shadow, Frank Asch, 1985.

Bridge to Terabithia, Katherine Paterson, 1977.

Brown Bear, Brown Bear, What Do You See?, Bill Martin, Jr., 1967.

Caddie Woodlawn, Carol Ryrie Brink, 1935.

Call of the Wild, Jack London, 1903.

Caps for Sale, Esphyr Slobodkina, 1940.

Charlotte's Web, E. B. White, 1952.

Chicka Chicka Boom Boom, Bill Martin, Jr. and John Archambault, 1989.

Corduroy, Don Freeman, 1968.

Dear Mr. Henshaw, Beverly Cleary, 1984.

Everybody Cooks Rice, Norah Dooley, 1991.

Five Little Monkeys series, Eileen Christelow, 1989.

Froggy Gets Dressed, Jonathan London, 1992.

Go, Dog. Go!, P. D. Eastman, 1961.

Goodnight Moon, Margaret Wise Brown, 1947.

Harriet the Spy, Louise Fitzhugh, 1964.

Hatchet, Gary Paulson, 1987.

If You Give A Mouse a Cookie, Laura Numeroff, 1985.

Ira Sleeps Over, Bernard Waber, 1972.

Island of the Blue Dolphins, Scott O'Dell, 1960.

James and the Giant Peach, Roald Dahl, *1961.*

Jesse Bear, What Will You Wear?, Nancy White Carlstrom, 1986.

Last Stop on Market Street, Matt de la Peña, 2015.

Leo the Late Bloomer, Robert Kraus, 1971.

Love You Forever, Robert Munsch, 1986.

Madeline, Ludwig Bemelmans, 1939.

Matilda, Roald Dahl, 1988.

Make Way for Ducklings, Robert McCloskey, 1941.

Millions of Cats, Wanda Gág, 1928.

Number the Stars, Lois Lowry, 1989.

Patty Reed's Doll: The Story of the Donner Party, Rachel K Laurgaard, 1989.

Rain, Robert Kalan, 1978.

Rosie's Walk, Pat Hutchins, 1968.

Sarah, Plain and Tall, Patricia MacLachlan, 1985.

Sign of the Beaver, Elizabeth George Speare, 1983.

Stellaluna, Janell Cannon, 1993.

Stone Fox, John Reynolds Gardiner, 1980.

Stone Soup, Ann McGovern, 1968.

Strega Nona, Tomie dePaola, 1975.

The Carrot Seed, Ruth Krauss, 1945.

The Lion, the Witch and the Wardrobe, C.S. Lewis, 1950.

The Little Engine That Could, Watty Piper (Arnold Munk) 1930.

The River (A Hatchet Adventure), Gary Paulsen, 1987.

The Snowy Day, Ezra Jack Keats, 1962.

The Very Hungry Caterpillar, Eric Carle, 1969.

Tikki Tikki Tembo, Arlene Mosel, 1968.

Tuck Everlasting, Natalie Babbitt, 1975.

Yo! Yes?, Chris Raschka, 2007.

About the Author

They call her 'Mrs. Words.' Rita Wirtz, an acclaimed teacher's coach, classroom teaching dynamo, reading specialist and consultant, received standing ovations and rave reviews wherever she appeared.

A sought-after keynote speaker and motivational performer, Ms. Wirtz presented her *Reading Champions! Easy-Start Reading* workshops across the United States. She also worked for several national seminar companies, offering teachers "The very best classroom-perfected reading strategies ever!"

Mrs. Wirtz, parent of four, taught language arts, English, speech, and reading at every skill level, preschool through adult, including lab, clinic, and classroom for more than forty years. She also worked as a K–6 and preschool principal, and at both county office and state department levels. Positions included curriculum consultant, literacy trainer, and Title I reading program evaluator.

With her vast practical experience and love of children, she really knows what works to teach all students to read or read better and faster. She is especially expert with underachieving children having reading challenges.

For many years, Rita taught reading courses for several universities and mentored a multitude of credential and student teachers. In addition, she taught school administration. Most significantly, she made weekly 'house calls' to schools, modeling reading strategies demonstration lessons in nearly six hundred K–12 classrooms. Rita routinely taught fundamental reading skills to learning-diverse students.

Mrs. Wirtz taught reading professionals, teachers, administrators, school board members, teaching assistants, parents, and tutors across the country. She keynoted for the California Department of Education, university commencements, and organizations such as Mentor Teachers, Early Childhood Education, Learning Disabilities groups, Special Education Program Specialists, Migrant Education/ Mini Corps, Bilingual, Child Welfare and Attendance, etc.

Rita currently volunteer teaches at preschool and public school, makes warmhearted special appearances, and writes. She lives in Eugene, Oregon.

Experience for yourself why thousands have flocked to Rita to catch her spirit and feel the joy of teaching students to be capable, confident readers. Most importantly, children of all ages became Reading Champs!

Rita's academic background includes a BA in English and speech, a reading specialist certification, a master's degree in reading, and an administrative services credential.

Other Writings by
Rita M. Wirtz, MA

Teaching for Achieving: How to Get the Achievement Results You Want. 1995.

K-3 Reading Success! Finding the Balance (What Works—How to Do It). 1996.

The Very Best Classroom-Tested Reading Strategies Ever! (Reading Success Recipes from 500 Classrooms). 1999.

Reading Champions! Master Training and Teaching Book. 2002.

Reading Champions! Teaching Reading Made Easy Video Set: Three Videos and Two Guidebooks. 2002.

"Creating Reading Champions!" (Newsletter article, CASCD), Foreword.

California Association for Supervision and Curriculum Development newsletter articles, (CASCD), Vol. 15, No. 3. 2002.

California English-Language Arts Standards (Correlations with Reading Champions!). 2002.

For Teachers and Administrators (Helping Students Meet Reading Standards). 2003.

50 Common Sense Reading Lessons (Reading success recipes for teachers, parents, classroom assistants and home schooling families). 2003.

Corrective Reading: Word Study. Reading Champions! Teaching Reading Made Easy (Steffen's Story), Teaching a "Left Behind" Child to Read). 2005.

Reading Champs, Teaching Reading Made Easy. LifeRich Publishing, 2014.

"Letter to Michigan Moms Who Love Reading," Guest article for *Michigan Mom Living, Homeschool.* June, 2016.

Fifty blogs on www.RitaWirtz.com. 2014-2018.

Featured Blogger, www.BAMRadioNetwork.com, with more than eighty blogs on EdWords. 2014-2018.

CPSIA information can be obtained
at www.ICGtesting.com
Printed in the USA
FFHW021519010519
52202410-57563FF